The Penland Book
of
Handmade Books

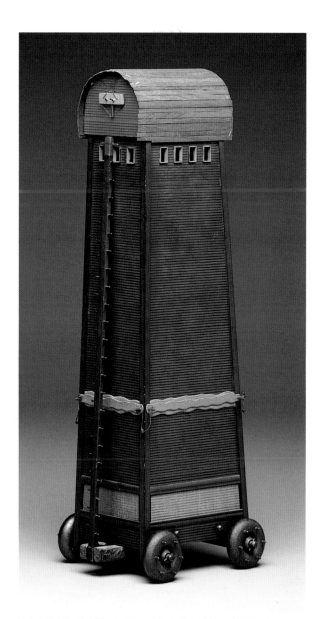

Dolph Smith, *First Wonder: Tennarkippi's Trojan House And The Secret Journal,* 1995. 5 x 29 x 8 inches (63.5 x 73.7 x 20.3 cm). Wood, acrylic, mixed media. The book is hidden under a false floor inside the movable tower. Collection of Dean and Kristi Jernigan. *Photo by Steve Mann.*

Dolph Smith, *First Wonder: Tennarkippi's Trojan House And The Secret Journal.*

The Penland Book
of
Handmade Books

Master Classes in
Bookmaking
Techniques

LARK BOOKS

A Division of Sterling Publishing Co., Inc.
New York / London

Editors: Jane LaFerla,
Veronika Alice Gunter

Art Director: Celia Naranjo

Photographer: Hands On
Photography by Steve Mann,
others listed on page 226

Cover Designer:
Barbara Zaretsky

Assistant Editor: Rebecca Guthrie

Associate Art Director:
Shannon Yokeley

Art Interns: Melanie Cooper
and Jason Thompson

Editorial Assistance: Delores
Gosnell, Rosemary Kast,
Jeff Hamilton

Proofreader: Valerie Anderson

The Library of Congress has cataloged the hardcover edition as follows:

The Penland book of handmade books : master classes in bookmaking techniques /
[Jane LaFerla and Veronika Alice Gunter, editors].
      p. cm.
  Includes index.
  ISBN 1-57990-474-2 (hardcover)
  1. Bookbinding—Handbooks, manuals, etc. 2. Books—Handbooks, manuals, etc.
  3. Bookbinding—Study and teaching. I. LaFerla, Jane. II. Gunter, Veronika Alice.
  III. Penland School of Crafts (Penland, N.C.) IV. Lark Books.

Z271.P45 2004
686.3--dc22

                                                                    2004007419

10 9 8 7 6 5 4 3 2

Published by Lark Books,
A Division of Sterling Publishing Co., Inc.
387 Park Avenue South, New York, N.Y. 10016

First Paperback Edition 2008
© 2004, Lark Books

Distributed in Canada by Sterling Publishing,
c/o Canadian Manda Group, 165 Dufferin Street
Toronto, Ontario, Canada M6K 3H6

Distributed in the United Kingdom by GMC Distribution Services,
Castle Place, 166 High Street, Lewes, East Sussex, England BN7 1XU

Distributed in Australia by Capricorn Link (Australia) Pty Ltd.,
P.O. Box 704, Windsor, NSW 2756 Australia

If you have questions or comments about this book, please contact:
Lark Books
67 Broadway
Asheville, NC 28801
(828) 253-0467

Manufactured in China
All rights reserved

ISBN 13: 978-1-57990-474-6 (hardcover) 978-1-60059-300-0 (paperback)
ISBN 10: 1-57990-474-2 (hardcover) 1-60059-300-3 (paperback)

For information about custom editions, special sales, premium and corporate purchases, please
contact Sterling Special Sales Department at 800-805-5489 or specialsales@sterlingpub.com.

Jim Croft, Untitled selection of books, 1991 to present. 3 x 4 x 2 to 5 x 7 x 2 (7 x 9.5 x 5 to 12.7 x 17.8 x 5 cm).
Handmade paper, brass, wood: California oak, Oregon maple, Oregon oak; carved fore-edge with carved cover.
Photo by Ralph Bartholdt.

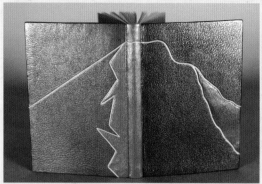

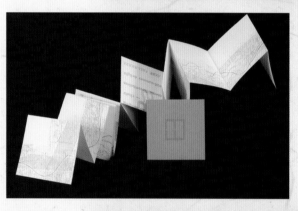

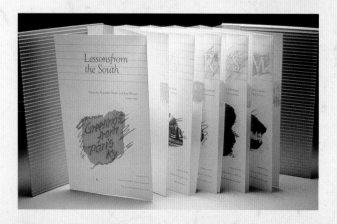

Contents

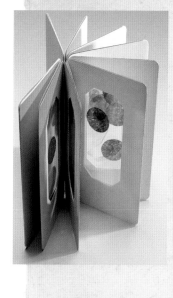

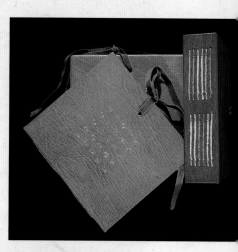

The Penland Book of Handmade Books is the second volume in the ongoing collaboration between Lark Books and Penland School of Crafts. Located 50 miles apart in the Appalachian mountains of Western North Carolina, Lark and Penland are almost neighbors, and this series of books brings together the complementary resources of our two institutions. Lark has years of experience producing a range of illustrated books designed to inspire readers

to work with their hands. Penland School of Crafts is a leader in craft education and has become a connection point for a national network of craft artists.

The chapters of this book were written by 10 book artists, each of them known for different techniques and ways of working; all of them have been instructors at Penland School. They were photographed demonstrating one of the techniques they use in their work and they wrote instructions to accompany these photographs. The artists also wrote an introductory essay talking about their technique, while touching on their professional history and sources of inspiration. In addition, artists also suggested gallery pieces to be featured by artists working with similar techniques.

Together, these 10 chapters constitute a technical and inspirational resource for intermediate to advanced practitioners. The book also demonstrates and documents a broad range of artists, ideas, and materials important to the contemporary practice of handmade books. The essays bring to the reader the voices and personalities of the individual artists. Their selection of work by other artists helps to broaden the reader's understanding of the topics and their range of possibilities.

The book is diverse, presenting traditional techniques along with approaches that challenge the very definition of what constitutes a book. This diversity is a strong reflection of the philosophy and content of Penland's program, not only in handmade books, but in all the areas covered by our classes. Book workshops at Penland may spend two intense weeks exploring one traditional bookbinding structure or they may present the student with a cornucopia of choices addressed by the teacher through individual instruction. Our classes have covered tool making for bookbinders, traditional bindings from a variety of cultures, miniature books, pop-up books, and the exploration of taking book structures into sculpture. We often have classes that use the materials of bookbinding to create boxes, slipcovers, and portfolios.

Books are tools for recording and transmitting ideas, information, images, and stories, and many of our classes focus on content as well as structure and technique. Book classes frequently include instruction in printmaking, drawing, writing, typography, letterpress printing, illumination, and other ways of generating material contained within the mechanisms of the book. Bookmaking classes often share resources and collaborate with the nearby printmaking and photography studios. Our instructors have approached the book as a cabinet of wonders, as an altar, as a reliquary, and as a portable studio. We have also found that children respond strongly to the act of making and the filling their own books, so handmade books have been an important part of our community education and teacher training classes.

Bookbinding was first taught at Penland in the 1930s as a casual addition to the regular program. It was not reintroduced as a regular offering until 1985. In 1991 a studio was built for classes in books and papermaking and these have been among Penland's most consistently popular offerings. Like many craft skills taught at Penland, hand bookbinding was once the standard technology of the time. Today, despite its obsolescence, it is an area of growing interest to both professional and avocational artists.

Penland attracts students and instructors from all over the country, and our book classes are taught by some the craft's finest practitioners. These instructors, like their students, value the retreat atmosphere, the egalitarian relationship between teachers and students, the intensity of the classes, and the teaching/learning model of the total-immersion workshop. Penland offers classes in ten areas, and our instructors often comment on the importance of interacting with colleagues working in other crafts and the opportunity to exchange ideas and information.

The excitement of a volume such as this one grows directly out of the vitality and creativity of contemporary book arts. Here you will find Jim Croft creating wooden covers and brass clasps for Gothic book structures while Daniel Essig uses some of the same techniques to create a haunting work of sculpture. Hedi Kyle shares the genesis of one of her innovative folded structures, and Eileen Wallace demonstrates the simplified binding—a traditional binding versatile in its applications. Steve Miller doesn't touch on book structures at all, choosing instead to focus on creating

imagery through a technique accessible to any bookbinder. Other chapters cover the "paper engineering" of pop-up books, the intimate connections between content and structure, the construction of elegant boxes, the relationship between books and sculpture, and structures that help reveal the layers of meaning found when presenting text in a visual format.

We are grateful to the artists/authors for their knowledge, their voices, and their beautiful and inspiring work. All of them have extended the reach of their work through teaching; this book will carry their contributions even farther. Thanks also go to Penland's program director Dana Moore who guided the content and served as Penland's point person, and to Rob Pulleyn, Jane LaFerla, Veronika Gunter, Celia Naranjo, and the staff of Lark Books who took the many pieces and made them into a book.

I hope and expect that this beautiful book will become a resource in your studio as you continue your exploration of the traditions and future of the handmade book.

Jean W. McLaughlin
Director, Penland School of Crafts

Daniel Essig

With the keen sensibility of a collector, Daniel Essig invites the reader into a wondrous cabinet of curiosities by incorporating found objects, such as fossils, arrowheads, and shells, into traditional book forms. His work draws us into an engaging space that is both familiar and transcendent, where we can explore and contemplate the cycle of life, death, and rebirth.

Niche Bridge Book, 2002.
23 x 16 x 6 inches
(57.5 x 40 x 15 cm).
Carved and painted
mahogany, spalted maple,
handmade flax paper,
1850s rag book pages,
linen thread, mica, bones,
and fossils; Ethiopian
binding. *Photo by
Walker Montgomery.*

Traces of the Past, Visions of the Future

Book of Nails, 2003, (open view, this page, closed view, next page). 7 x 11 x 17 inches (17.5 x 27.5 x 42.5 cm) (opened). Carved and painted mahogany, handmade flax paper, tin, velvet, linen thread, mica, nails, trilobite fossils; Ethiopian binding.
Photo by Walker Montgomery.

Some people use my books as journals and fill them up with words. I don't write in my books. For me, the books themselves are journals—visual records of my life and work. I am interested in traces of the past—ancient binding styles, altered books, distressed finishes, and found objects. I've developed my style of bookmaking by learning from mentors and absorbing the influence of treasured objects from other cultures and other times.

Since I was six or seven years old, I've been collecting small objects. I have seashells that I collected at the beach on childhood vacations, dried sea horses, starfish, and mineral collections that I bought at gift shops. I've always picked up interesting rocks, and I also have my grandfather's arrowhead collection. He lived in central Missouri, and he walked the freshly plowed fields collecting these stone relics of the land's past inhabitants. I've stored up seed pods, rocks,

bones, shells, bits of rusty metal, nails, animal teeth, and fossils. They represent periods in my life, even just days or moments—a family vacation, or a walk through the woods with friends. I also have many objects that people have sent me; they find things that remind them of me, and these things in turn remind me of them. Sometimes friends collect objects as souvenirs for themselves, then turn them over to me when they want to forget those particular times.

I also pick up dead cicadas, and there are often a couple of them drying out on the dashboard of my truck. The idea of the life cycle—of metamorphosis—recurs frequently in my work, and the cicada is a good symbol of this. As a child at my grandma's house in the country I found the loud buzzing noise of cicadas very comforting, and I collected the molted shells that I found clinging to the trunks of trees. Later I learned that juvenile cicadas—called

DANIEL ESSIG

trips with them, and we traveled all over the Southeast looking for salamanders and insects and small fish. I went along mostly to photograph the sites, but I also helped pull the nets and catch the insects. One of my photography professors, Chuck Swedlund, hired me as his graduate assistant on photographic caving expeditions. I carried equipment, held strobes, and fired off flash bulbs for Chuck and other cave photographers. For several months we worked almost every day underground. During the long stretches of inactivity, I searched for fossils and cave life and took photographs of my own. I also spent a lot of time wandering above ground, collecting images of melting ice, weathered rocks, eroding soil, and rotting trees. I gravitate toward the colors of decay, the beauty of aging. I kept an eye out for Native American petroglyphs—abstract designs or images of footprints or animals—and became good at finding them.

Medieval Spirit of the Times, 2003. 29 x 18 x 4½ inches (12.5 x 10 x 6.25 cm). Oak, deer leather, linen rope, sinew, 1850s rag newspaper, mica, snail shell, ammonite fossil; Gothic binding.
Photo by Walker Montgomery.

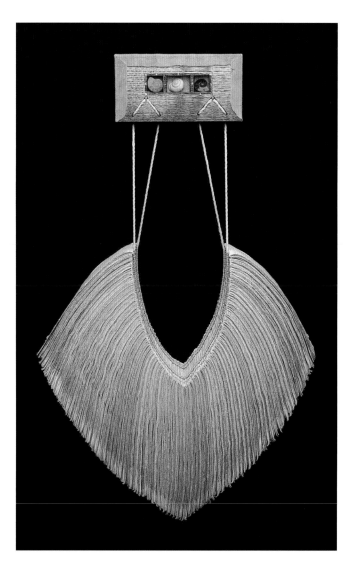

nymphs—live underground around a tree for years, then tunnel out and crawl into the tree, where they molt and begin calling for mates. The females lay their eggs on the tree branches, and when the eggs hatch the nymphs fall to the ground and burrow underground. The life cycle of a cicada revolves around a tree. I make my book covers out of trees, of course, and I sometimes use cicada shells and the dead insects themselves to represent the cycle of life, death, and rebirth.

I keep my collection of objects in various cabinets, drawers, bottles, and boxes within a single small room in my house. The space has the feel of a German *Wunderkammern,* a "cabinet of curiosity." I sit in the room and scan my collection for just the right object for each of my books and sculptures.

I got into bookmaking while studying at the University of Southern Illinois in Carbondale. Although I was majoring in photography, I found kinship with the science graduate students. I went on collecting

Archeologists, who keep certain locations secret, were surprised that I had discovered unpublished sites. These places were sacred to me.

Rather than framing my photographs and mounting them on walls, I decided to place them in boxes or books so that the viewer had to actively explore them, rather than just wandering past. On one occasion I found a little newt—a red eft—that had been flattened by a car on the road. He was dry, curled up, and so paper-thin that I preserved him between two sheets of handmade paper and mounted him in a book. It was a sort of petroglyph. I made one of my first books, before I knew how to bind, as an altered book. It was printed in Greek. I glued the pages together, and they were so brittle that I could scrape out an Indian marking that I often saw in Southern Illinois.

Around this time, I visited my sister in Iowa City, Iowa, and met a friend of hers named Al Buck, who was making wooden-covered Coptic books. The binding was first used around the 4th century, in Ethiopia or North Africa—or perhaps this is just the area where the books were best preserved. What first appealed to me about Coptic books was that, unlike most hand-bound books, they open completely flat. When I put images on the pages, you could see the whole image without struggling with the binding. Al sent me a book that he had made, along with handwritten instructions. Since I knew nothing about book making—or sewing, or paper, or woodworking—it was a challenge. There are holes drilled vertically through the board, but other holes are drilled at angles from the edge of the board to both the inside and outside face. This perplexed me. I didn't know whether to hold the board in a vice at an angle or to use a drill press. Al told me to clamp the board to the inside of a drawer, and then drill the hole with a hand drill, just eyeballing it. I thought I would have to use a power tool, and I was happy to learn that it was easiest to drill the holes with a simple tool that my grandfather could have used. (I now use a metalsmith's power drill called a flexshaft, but I still eyeball the angle.) Once I mastered the drilling, the rest of the process fell into place. Still, it took me nearly two years to make a book I was satisfied with.

My first book arts mentor was Frances Lloyd Swedlund, who at the time was a cinema and photography graduate student at the University of Southern Illinois. She also made exquisitely crafted books. A lot of people were impressed with the first boxes and books that I made, but Frances was not. The others liked the simple fact that I was making boxes and books; she saw that they were sloppily made, with no sense of craftsmanship. Frances, who had studied at Penland, knew that that would be the place for me to learn bookmaking, and she urged Chuck (who had taught at Penland himself) to send me there. Chuck was reluctant to lose his assistant (after all, somebody had to haul his equipment through the cave muck), but ultimately he agreed. So as I finished my degree at Carbondale, I spent my summers as a work scholarship student at Penland, and later I became a core student there. (Core students are year-round work-study scholarship students.) It was at Penland that I began to concentrate exclusively on Coptic books.

There are several distinct sewings called Coptic. I refer to the style I use as Ethiopian. I use two needles for each length of thread, one on either end. I use wood covers and tunnel through the edge of the board to attach the text block. The combination of the historic sewing style, wooden boards, and the type of board attachment are what distinguish the Ethiopian binding.

One of the first people I met at Penland was Julie Leonard, who was a resident artist at Penland at the time. I assisted in her classes, and she helped me learn how to make a living by making production journals. These are still one-of-a-kind books, but I can make them fairly quickly and sell them for a reasonable price at craft shows. I've made hundreds over the years, and I can't imagine stopping now. I spend so much of my time sewing books that the process is meditative. It gives me an opportunity to think about the structure of the book, and how to stretch the limits of the Coptic form.

Dolph Smith helped push me beyond the simple Ethiopian book. He was making sculptural books by hanging paper from wooden structures, and I tracked him down and ultimately studied with him. Under his

influence I developed my bridge books. They use the same Coptic binding but exaggerate each of the elements: the covers become elongated into 2-foot-long (60 cm) towers that stand on a tabletop, and rather than 10 or 12 signatures in the text block, I use 100 to 200—well over 1,000 pages. I can't afford that much paper, so to make the bridges I return to the idea of the altered book. I find books that have mangled spines and covers but good quality paper, and I use that paper in my work. Often I use old bibles with exceptionally thin paper, which has a nice drape and flow. One of my favorite things about bookbinders is listening to them justify tearing up old books. I don't have much of a problem with this, because the books I alter are not rare, and they've lived their lives. Bookbinders have been recycling books for 2,000 years. In some of the first Coptic books, wood was scarce, and the binders would take old papyrus scrolls and laminate many layers together to make book covers that are close to an inch (2.5 cm) thick.

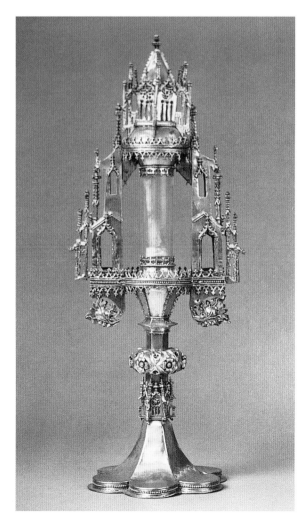

Monstrance with a Relic of St. Sebastian, Germany, Lower Saxony, Brunswick, c. 1475. Height 58 inches (147 cm). Gilt silver and rock crystal.

The Cleveland Museum of Art, Gift of Julius F. Goldschmidt, Z.M. Hackenbroch, and J. Rosenbaum in memory of the Exhibition of the Guelph Treasure held in the Cleveland Museum of Art from 10 January to 1 February 1931, 31.65.

Sacred Geometry, the book I demonstrate in the Hands On section, is typical of the work I do now. It draws inspiration from a number of sources, including medieval reliquaries (see page 15) and African nail figures (below), and, as with all my work, it has an Ethiopian book at its heart. Rather than stretch the elements of the book, as with the bridge books, I make a fairly standard small book the centerpiece of a work of sculpture.

As I see it, a well-designed, well-crafted miniature book can have as much power as a large-scale work. I like to start with an object and then build a book or sculpture around it. For *Sacred Geometry* I chose a trilo-bite. This particular fossil has the practical advantage of being thin enough to fit in the cover of a book, but there is more to it than that. There is something miraculous about a fragile living creation being transformed into a timeless rock and preserved for hundreds of millions of years. I like to think of my books and sculptures as reliquaries, containers for the sacred remains of the past.

After choosing the object, I chose wood for the covers. In this case I used mahogany, because it is wonderful to work with. Changes in humidity can cause many woods to swell, shrink, or bend, which can stress the binding, but mahogany is very stable. With oak, the drill bit and chisel tend to run with the grain, and maple is hard to carve into. Mahogany is almost perfect. It doesn't chip or splinter, and it takes easily to the chisel. It's almost like working with frozen butter. Since I was trying to create something that appears to be hundreds of years old, I knew mahogany, once I distressed it, would have the look I wanted.

I use mica, a silicate mineral that crystallizes into thin, transparent leaves, for my windows. Mica is a forgiving material; it can be drilled and cut and will not shatter or break. Because I want my books to be touched as well as viewed, creating tactile contrast is important to me. For *Sacred Geometry,* I attached rusted tin salvaged from an old barn to the covers—the rusted metal nicely complemented the rich colors of the boards.

The paper, salvaged from a water-damaged book dated 1790, is strong and flexible, a cream white, pulled by hand, and made with very pure water. The paper is mostly blank, because I cut it from

N'kisi Nkonde Figure, late 19th century. From Congo Brazzaville, Africa. 15¾ x 9¾ x 7¼ inches (40 x 24.8 x 18.4 cm). Wood, natural fibers, nails. *Courtesy of the Minneapolis Institute of Arts, The Christina N. and Swan J. Turnblad Memorial Fund.*

Centipede Binding, 2003 (open view). 5 x 4 x 2½ inches (12.5 x 10 x 6.25 cm). Mahogany, milk paint, walnut-stained handmade flax paper. Italian handmade paper, linen thread, brass, leather, mica, fossils; Greek and centipeded binding. *Photo by Walker Montgomery.*

the undamaged margins of the book, but it does contain a few words, because the original book's notes were printed in the margins. Also, I used the red-stained fore-edge of the original book as the top edge of my miniature book. This red accentuates the oxblood of the boards, and, together with marginal notes, hints at the paper's former life in a different book.

Bookbinders once attached linen cord and bits of leather under the leather of the cover to build up a design. In a similar way, I glued cord and leather to the top of the arch I cut. By covering the design with a piece of walnut-stained, handmade flax paper, which I dipped in gelatin sizing to make it stronger and water resistant, the leather and cords underneath blended into one design. I coated the paper with milk paint, an ancient type of paint made from milk protein, lime, clay, and earth pigment, applying five coats in yellow, orange, green, red. Once the final coat was dry, sanding into the paint allowed each of the colors to come out. After distressing, I affixed the nails, having scavenged many of them from a burned-down barn in New Hampshire, though a few came from contemporary makers of traditional nails.

The most striking aspect of *Sacred Geometry* is the halo of nails, which I borrowed from *n'kisi nkondi* nail figures, wooden sculptures made by the Kongo peoples of central Africa and used for protecting the village, curing illnesses, and settling disputes. Inside a cavity in the figure's head or stomach were placed ritual substances, such as herbs, animal bones, fur, and seeds—a detail similar to my own use of found objects. Each of the nails driven into a n'kisi figure represents one occasion when the power of the figure was invoked.

To me, the nails also suggest a defense, like the quills of a porcupine. In medieval Europe, books were so rare and precious that they were chained to library shelves, and in some of my work I chain books to niches, or chain smaller books to larger books, to suggest their preciousness. In *Sacred Geometry*, it is the nails that provide the protection.

DANIEL ESSIG

Hands On

Daniel demonstrates making the book Sacred Geometry, step-by-step, from the initial block of wood to the weathered-looking finished piece.

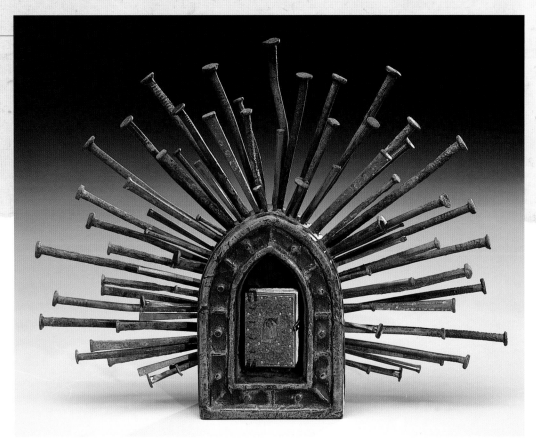

Books as Sculpture

1. A compass, pencil, and ruler determine the layout of the arch and the niche within the arch.

2. After removing the bulk of the wood with a forstner drill bit, a chisel cleans up and defines the cutout.

3. A smaller chisel carves and rounds the edges of the arch.

4. A piece of cord is wrapped around the arch near the front edge of the piece and secured with glue. After laying out a design on the arch, I cut short lengths of cord and punch out tiny rounds of leather to use in the design. After applying glue in the places where the materials will be attached, I use tweezers to place the pieces of cord and leather.

5. A foam brush applies glue to the arch for securing the paper in place. The paper needs to be secure since it will be painted and sanded in later steps.

6. After applying the paper, I use two bone folders to outline the cord that was wrapped around the arch. The outlining defines the cord so it won't be lost under the layer of paper.

7. I apply five coats of milk paint to the piece, letting each coat of paint dry before applying the next one.

8. Waiting for each coat of paint to dry gives me time to begin work on the book that will inhabit the niche within the arch. I cut the wood pieces that will serve as the cover, then drill holes in the covers to accommodate the binding.

9. Drilling is done at an angle, from the edge of the wood to the edge of the cover.

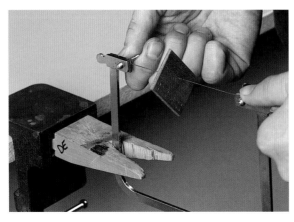

10. A jeweler's saw cuts the window in the cover, which will hold the trilobite. It's important to tighten the saw blade before sawing.

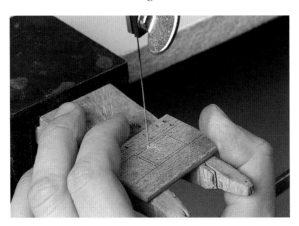

11. The fine cuts in the delicate cover piece can also be made with the jeweler's saw.

12. I use a stain marker to apply stain to the covers.

13. A small chisel smoothes the shelf that will hold the piece of mica that serves as the windowpane.

14. After peeling off one layer of mica to remove any surface scratches, I use a cutting tool to cut two identical pieces of mica—one for each side of the window.

15. The nail holes that will hold one of the mica pieces in place are pre-punched in each corner of the shelf. I use tweezers to insert each nail, then a small hammer taps each in place.

17. Tin snips cut out two pieces of rusted tin—one will be attached to the front cover and the other to the back. Working on a piece of scrap wood and using an old chisel and hammer, I cut a window in the piece for the front cover. When the book is finished, this window allows the reader to see the mica and the trilobite.

18. Holes are pre-drilled for the nails that will hold the tin pieces in place. Tweezers hold the small nails while I tap them in. Attaching a piece of leather to the inside of the back cover and a pin in the front cover makes the closure.

16. I sort through my selection of found objects to find the right one to inhabit the books. After a trilobite is selected, the front cover is flipped over and the trilobite inserted from the backside. Then, I attach a second piece of mica as I did in step 15.

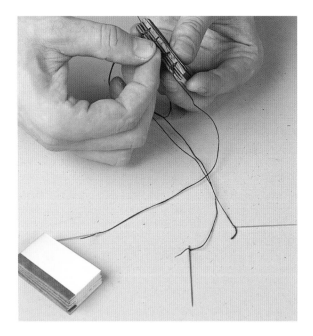

20. Distressing the arch exposes the layers of paint and is done by sanding with 220-grit sandpaper—sometimes I use a power sander. I sand until I'm satisfied with the appearance.

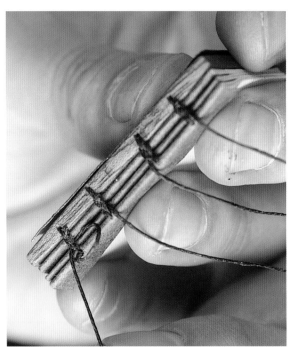

21. Burnishing the paint is done with #0000 steel wool; then a soft cloth is used to dust the surface.

19. For binding the folios of the book, I use two needles for each length of thread, one on either end. The text block attaches to the cover by tunneling through the edge of each board.

22. The arch gets an application of oxblood shoe polish. After application, I buff the arch with a paper towel.

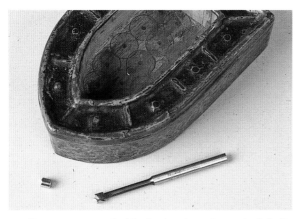

23. Since a magnet holds the book in the arch, I drill a hole that will secure the magnet in place. The magnet will be covered with velvet.

24. To cover the inside of the niche, a piece of velvet is cut to size and attached to the niche using double-sided tape. Distressing the edges of the velvet is easier if you do it before adhering it in the niche.

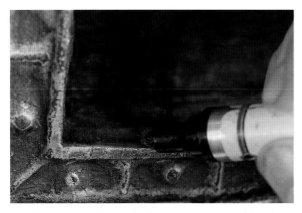

25. Using a marker with the same stain used for the book's covers, I outline the distressed edges of the velvet.

26. Using a drill with a #30 bit, I install a hanging mechanism on the back. It's made of some cord and wood wedges that will secure the cord in place.

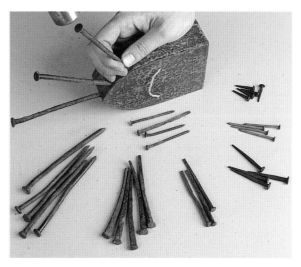

27. I choose an assortment of nails to adorn the outside edges of the arch. After pre-drilling holes for the nails, I place a drop of glue in each hole before inserting each nail. A hammer taps the nails in place—sometimes several taps are needed.

About the Artist

DANIEL ESSIG works out of studios located at Grovewood Gallery and Cyclone Enterprises in Asheville, NC, where he is also a member of Ariel Gallery, a cooperative fine art gallery.

A recipient of a 2002 North Carolina Visual Artist Fellowship, Daniel regularly teaches at Penland School of Crafts, Arrowmont Craft School, and John C. Campbell Folk School. He has also taught at Pyramid Atlantic, North Country Studio Conference, Meredith College, Webster University, Garage Annex School of Book Arts, Minnesota Center for Book Arts, and the University of Iowa Center for the Book.

Daniel's work has appeared in exhibits at the Mint Museum, the Academy of Natural Sciences, Southern Alleghenies Museum of Art, the Houston Center for Contemporary Craft, the Fuller Museum of Art, Wyoming University, Blue Spiral Gallery, and T&E Gallery in Vienna. He has shown and sold art at several juried craft shows, including the Smithsonian Craft Show, Philadelphia Museum of Art Craft Show, American Craft Exposition, the American Craft Council, and Craft Boston.

His sculptures and books have been featured in Keith Smith's *Structure of the Visual Book* and *Non-Adhesive Bindings, Vols. 3 and 4*; Suzanne J. E. Tourtillott's *The New Photo Craft* and *Making and Keeping Creative Journals*; and in the magazines *American Craft*, *American Style*, *Crafts Reports*, and *FIBERARTS*.

Gallery

I am amazed by the variety of structural ingenuity that is inspired by the basic book form. My gallery includes books that have invited me to explore their contents. Each book beckons to be handled, and the reward is the sighting of a hidden world. In Keith Lo Bue's book, a former photo album is now a shrine filled with a brooch—and the haunting smell of old paper and of the anise pods that have been tucked inside. In Francis Swedlund's books, an unassuming exterior reveals a complex layering of photos and found objects that hint at a personal story. Pamela Spitzmueller reveals a hidden book in a fold of fabric reminiscent of a medieval girdle book. Robyn Raines has bound a number of books together to create a new form that is organic and refined, yet retains the simple concept of cover and page. Matthew Thomason has turned the Coptic binding into an elaborate structure that encircles the lip of a teacup. Brooke Spurlock has constructed an elegant and whimsical book that is read by rotating the Ferris wheel. Shanna Leino's exquisite bone carving and bindings have transformed historical structures into masterpieces that are remarkable for their craft and beauty. Dolph Smith's striking bridge book was the initial inspiration for my sculptural books.

I have also included the work of three sculptors. The distressed surface of Hoss Haley's steel sphere looks as though it has been weathering for years. The industrial rivets are a sharp contrast to the polished mahogany of Kurt Neilsen's Minotaur. *Kurt's ability to animate wood with life and playfulness continues to inform and inspire my work. Chris Ramsay's shell-encrusted plate speaks of a reverence to the natural world that is a basic element in each of my books.*

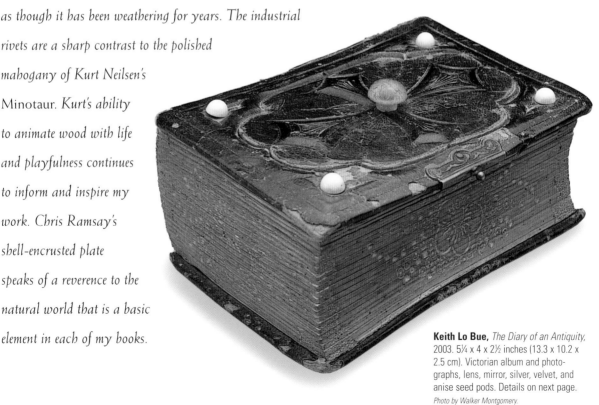

Keith Lo Bue, *The Diary of an Antiquity,* 2003. 5¼ x 4 x 2½ inches (13.3 x 10.2 x 2.5 cm). Victorian album and photographs, lens, mirror, silver, velvet, and anise seed pods. Details on next page.
Photo by Walker Montgomery.

Keith Lo Bue, *The Diary of an Antiquity,*
2003. 5¼ x 4 x 2½ inches (13.3 x 10.2 x 2.5
cm). Victorian album and photographs, lens,
mirror, silver, velvet, and anise seed pods.
Photos by Walker Montgomery.

Robyn Raines, *The Atomic Nucleus,* 2003. 15 x 10 x 7 inches (37.5 x 25 x 17.5 cm).
Altered books, linen thread, wood; Coptic binding; piece is freestanding in many different positions. *Photo by Kyung Cho.*

DANIEL ESSIG

Chris Ramsay, *Endangered,* 2001. 15 x 12 x 11 inches (37.5 x 30 x 27.5 cm). 1950's reclaimed globe, international postage stamps, illustrations, cast resin, bronze, steel, found objects. *Photos by the artist.*

Frances L. Swedlund, *The Messenger,* 1989. 10½ x 8 x 2½ inches (26.7 x 20.3 x 6.4 cm). Victorian photo album, silver print, dead bird, map, bone, shells; cab driver hat buttons, and other found objects. *Photo by the artist.*

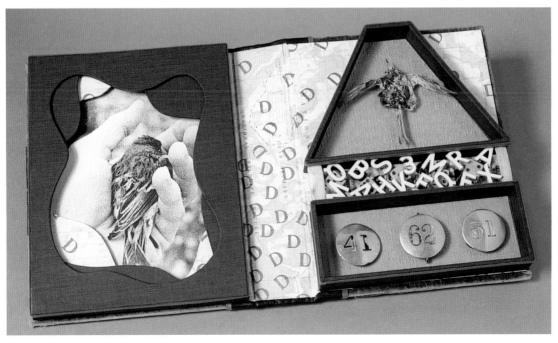

Shanna Leino, *Book for Dan,* 2000. 1½ x 2½ inches (3.8 x 6.25 cm). Carved elk bone, flax, paper, linen thread. *Photo by Walker Montgomery.*

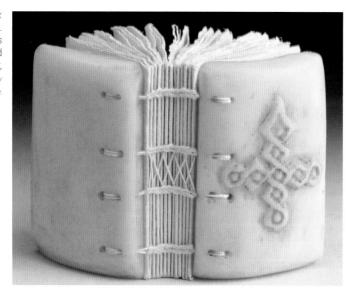

Matthew Thomason in collaboration with **Meredith Brickell,** *Teacup,* 2001. 8 x 8 x 3 inches (20 x 20 x 7.5 cm). Handmade flax paper; Coptic binding with linen thread; wheel-thrown porcelain; cone 10. *Photos by Tom Mills.*

Pamela Spitzmueller, *Fresh Pearls,* 1999. 12 x 6 x 8 inches (30 x 15 x 20 cm). Wood and deerskin cover; textile overcover embellished with freshwater pearls; bone ring for gripping and carrying book as in medieval girdle books. *Photo by the artist.*

Kurt Nielsen, *Guardian Dog Credenza,* 2000. 48 x 60 x 18 inches (120 x 150 x 45 cm). Madrone burl, maple, linden; bent lamination, bookmatched veneer; dogs hand carved; traditional woodworking joinery. *Photos by David Ramsey.*

Kurt Nielsen, *Minotaur Morning,* 2001. 34 x 36 x 20 inches (85 x 90 x 50 cm). Mahogany, African satinwood, pommelle sapele; 14k gold; bent lamination; bookmatched veneer; minotaurs hand carved; horns and nose rings sculpted in wax then molded and cast in solid 14K gold. *Photos by David Ramsey.*

Robyn Raines, *Bottle Cap Books,* 2003. 1 x 1 x ½ inches (2.5 x 2.5 x 1.3 cm). Magazine paper, bottle caps, wire; Coptic bound using floral wire. *Photo by Kyung Cho.*

Hoss Haley, *Red Sphere,* 2003. 24 inches (dia.) (60 cm). Enamel paint on steel. *Photo by Ken Pitts.*

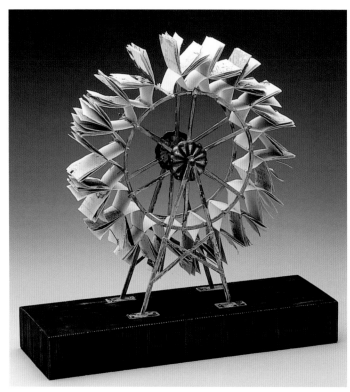

Brook Spurlock, *Ferris Wheel,* 2003. 8 x 12 x 4 inches (20.3 x 30.5 x 10.2 cm). Handmade flax and mica paper, cyanotypes, linen thread, copper, gesso, color pencil ebonized maple. *Photos by Walker Montgomery.*

Chris Ramsay, *Fossils: Patterns of Organic Energy,* 1993. 24 inches (diameter) x 12 inches (60 x 30 cm). Found objects, fossils, shells, wood; copper-patina. *Photos by the artist.*

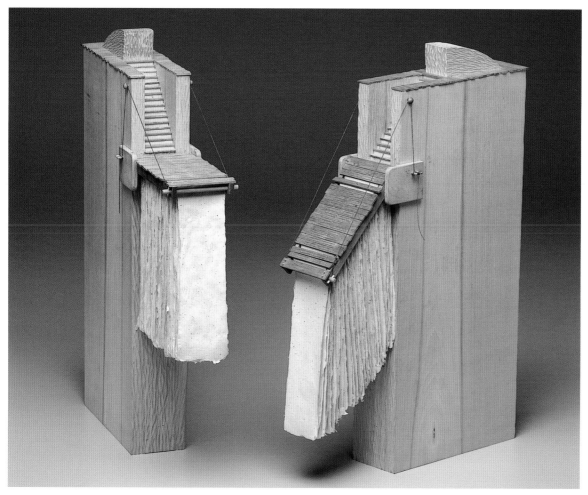

Dolph Smith, *Tennarkippi's Bridge of Peace,* 1993. 27 x 33 x 3½ inches (68.6 x 83.8 x 8.9 cm). Wood, handmade paper. *Photo by Steve Mann.*

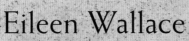

Eileen Wallace

In her refined version of the simplified binding, Eileen Wallace presents a versatile structure that works well with a variety of cover materials—from paper to metal. The technique allows the cover boards to be prepared separately from the spine, giving the artist more freedom to explore decorative cover applications such as tooling and the use of onlays.

Matched, 2003. 7 x 8 x ⅝ inches (17.5 x 20 x 1.6 cm). Leather, paper, board, printed paper of vintage matchbox labels from artist's collection; simplified binding. *Photo by the artist.*

The pages of the text block

Inside of back cover

The Elegance of Simplicity

The Strange Case of Dr. Jekyll and Mr. Hyde, by Robert Louis Stevenson,1994. Wood engravings by Barry Moser. 4½ x 6½ inches (11.3 x 16.3 cm). University of Nebraska Press, Pennyroyal Press edition. Leather, board, gilded graphite edges, paper; full-leather simplified binding with onlays.
Photo by Robert Chiarito.

By a string of seemingly unrelated events, I've ended up making books. When I look back I can see how it happened. I like order and have for as long as I can remember. Childhood photographs show my dolls sleeping in a perfect line and knickknacks arranged precisely on my shelves. But I also know I have a high tolerance for disorder.

I tend to clean my workspace before beginning a job, but by the end of the day I am working on about one-quarter of my table as the rest is completely cluttered. A friend once told me that he liked coming to my house because you could never be sure if it would be perfectly neat or look as if a tornado came through. It seems to be one extreme or the other.

In college, my mother gave me a copy of *The Robber Bridegroom* by Eudora Welty, which led me to pay much more attention to the details of books. This particular book was the offset version of The Pennyroyal Press edition designed and illustrated by Barry Moser.

I am not sure what I noticed first, but I know it was the first time I remember looking at a book and thinking "This is a beautiful book."

I've always been interested in art, but I don't draw or paint. It wasn't until graduate school that I realized that this lack of skill didn't mean I couldn't have a creative life. My journey to actually making books began with research on where to go for a Masters in Library Service. I intended to make a career of doing research and, fortunately, I landed at the University of Alabama School of Library and Information Studies that also houses the M.F.A. in the Book Arts Program. I remember thinking, "That sounds like what I want to do, but I can't draw, I'm not an artist, I can't get in."

I thought I'd go for my library degree and perhaps take a few classes to see what the book program was all about. I wasn't on campus a month before I applied to the program. I had long appreciated fine paper, printing, and bookbinding, but honestly, it never occurred to me that I could actually make a book. I'd never been exposed to fine press books and I just didn't know it was an option. I found I fit right in to the traditional craft-based program. I have patience for tedious detail, but I can also envision a completed project as a whole.

In the development of my book career, I've come back to the things that first attracted me to books. I'm interested in how we communicate, how we mark time and record events. I'm interested in the graphic representation of these through alphabetic, symbolic, and logographic writing systems. Early illuminated manuscripts with Islamic patterns and Celtic interlocking designs were an initial fascination, but I was quickly enamored with simpler and bolder forms of writing. The Ogham writing system of the ancient Celts is a series of lines and dashes similar to hatch marks and is one of my favorite methods of record keeping. Cuneiform, the Etruscan alphabet, and early Ethiopian script are all writing systems that I find visually intriguing.

It's not the actual language nor the words that are attractive to me, but rather the construction and organization of the written symbols that create pattern and give rhythm to the page—the act of putting random marks on a page that somehow come together in recognizable forms. While I may have first noticed it with letters and words, the idea of pattern and rhythm is present in all of my work. As I take a critical look at my own work and also evaluate the things that appeal to me, I find myself visually interested in an imposed order on chaos, and it's this combination of elements that I find most exciting. I see it in the way a diamond-patterned fence creates a grid over a wall of peeling paint or the way rows of crops flash by in a flurry of lines as you drive by a field.

But even beyond something recognizable, I've always been interested in marks that create pattern or texture and that's what interests me the most—especially when it has a sense of history or unintentional beauty. I see it in rust on a cotton combine or peeling paint layers on a building. And I see it in color—the color of freshly plowed Mississippi Delta dirt and the spring green of leaves on a Ginkgo tree. I finally realized that this is enough for me. I don't have to be able to render a perfect portrait in order to be an artist or

craftsman. More importantly, I've learned that I don't want to be able to do this.

By necessity, bookbinding and printing are very precise crafts. To me, a book is a sequence of detailed steps that build upon each other to create the "big picture." It's my goal to combine these details to make books that are cohesive in design and decoration. This doesn't mean that the content or decoration need be rigid but the actual processes demand precision in order to be done well. At one point I thought I'd made a big mistake since there are some steps in bookbinding that I don't find terribly exciting—folding signatures and tearing paper for editions, for instance. But I make it through these steps because it's the process as a whole that I find enjoyable. For me, it's the process of making a book work physically.

There's a constant struggle in me between the idea of content and structure. When I was first learning, I spent a lot of time on structure. I didn't experiment with content or decoration until I knew that my structure was right in that the book opened and closed properly, that my joint spaces were correct, etc. I never want decoration or embellishment to

Untitled, 1997. 5½ x 7 inches (13.8 x 17.5 cm). Recycled copper roofing, rivets, leather, paper; simplified binding (modified). *Photo by Steve Yusko.*

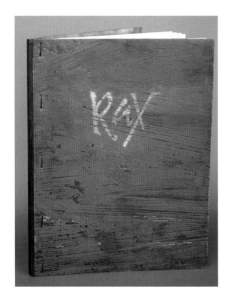

A Note on the Type, by Ron Carlson, 1996. Calligraphy by Glenn Epstein 7¼ x 9½ x ⅜ inches (18 x 23.8 x .95 cm). Mile Wide Press, printed by Eileen Wallace. Recycled metal roofing, leather, paper, wax; letterpress printing from lead type and magnesium engravings; simplified binding with lettering scratched into the cover. *Photo by Robert Chiarito.*

compensate for any shortcomings in structure. When I teach bookbinding, I try to pass along this strategy to students. I also tell them that they can choose not to follow my guidelines as long as they're making an informed decision. While I think you should experiment with materials, you should do so in a way that manages to create a cohesive structure where the materials make sense with the content or intent of the structure.

I like the challenge of making a book open well, but I also like to push the limits of flexibility and usability. In general, I like sewing structures that are mechanical, relying on paper, thread, and sometimes supports to do the work. I don't mind seeing how it's held together. At the same time, there's a side of me

that craves elegance and simplicity and a little bit of mystery. This is why the simplified-style binding is a perfect blend of my particular binding interests.

I first experienced the Simplified structure in graduate school after my professor learned of the technique from the innovator of the binding, Sün Evrard. In reality, there's not anything simple about the Simplified except that it's less involved than most French fine-binding techniques. Over the years, I have returned to this structure many times and I have refined it even further to fit my particular needs.

When I was planning the binding for the book *A Note on the Type,* I had the good luck of stumbling upon many sheets of old tin roofing material that had been painted red and were now rusty and showing signs of

Count Me If You Can, 2002. 5½ x 6½ x ½ inches (13.8 x 16.3 x 1.3 cm). Cloth, board; monoprint; handwriting; found images on paper; accordion binding. *Photo by the artist.*

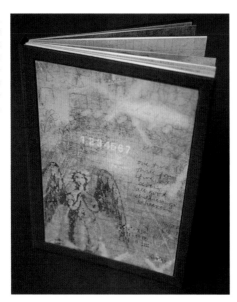

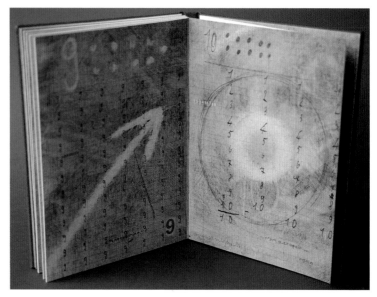

EILEEN WALLACE

Untitled, 1998. Collaboration with Hoss Haley. 6½ x 7 x 1 inches (16.3 x 17.5 x 2.5 cm). Steel, leather, paper; modified simplified/ split board. *Photo by the artist.*

binding was the answer. From this point I better understood the potential of the structure. The flexibility this structure allows is its most appealing feature. It can be full leather; it can be a combination of leather and paper, cloth and paper, leather and metal, and almost any permutation of these materials and others not listed. The beauty of it compared to a full-leather tight back, for instance, is that the cover boards are prepared separately from the spine and attached later. This means you can tool designs or apply onlays to your boards without having the covers already attached to the book.

The Simplified structure is best for slim volumes. Though the outer appearance is clean and elegant, there are many steps that go into making it appear so simple. Beveled boards, perfectly pared leather, and sanded seams are some of the steps that enhance the beauty and appeal of this structure. You can make this book as refined as the full-leather or less fancy with paper and cloth.

For me, the greatest appeal is the option to attach a variety of cover materials to the spine piece. The simplified binding allows me to use the techniques and materials I prefer for making the books I enjoy.

wear. It was a perfect cover material for this quirky story about a car thief who has a history of scratching his name, Ray, in most any metal surface he can find.

I set about trying to figure out how to use this metal on the book so it made sense and wasn't just some piece of metal stuck on a cover. After several models, I realized that a version of the simplified

Untitled blank journal, 1996-1997. 5¼ x 6¼ (12.8 x 15.6 cm). Recycled metal roofing, acrylics, spray paint, wax, leather, paper; Simplified binding (modified). *Photo by Robert Chiarito.*

Hands On

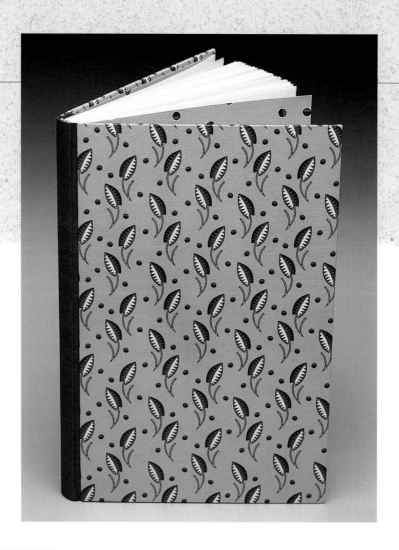

Eileen demonstrates the steps to her refined version of the simplified binding.

Simplified Binding

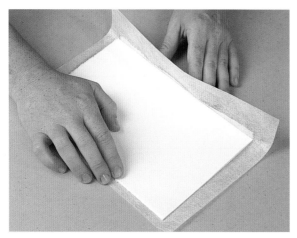

1. Japanese paper reinforces the outer folio of the first and last signatures. Pasting Japanese paper, and folding it with the aid of a piece of nonwoven interfacing, such as Remay or Pellon, prevents the paper from sticking, and allows me to wrap the outside of the signature with ease. The Japanese paper is pasted with a 50/50 mixture of PVA and methylcellulose.

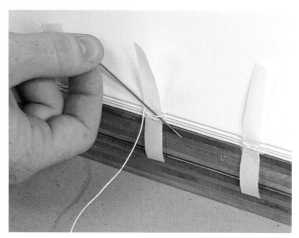

2. After the signatures are dry, they're collated and the sewing holes are punched. I punch three sewing stations for the sewing tapes. I find that Ramie brand tapes work best because they are flat and can be frayed out later. The signatures are sewn using the French linking stitch with the kettle stitch at the change over.

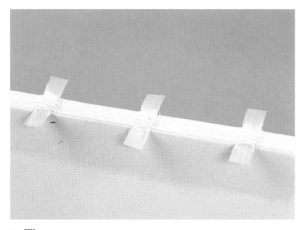

3. The sewn signatures

4. Once the book is sewn, the spine is glued up with PVA.

5. With the glue partially dry but still tacky, I use a hammer to gently round the spine.

6. I always look for other steps to do while waiting for glue to dry. Here, I make temporary beveled boards that will protect the book in its various stages of completion. A scalpel makes the shallow bevel that will remove about one-half the board's thickness.

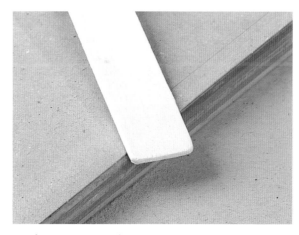

7. After cutting, sanding blocks or sticks smooth out the bevel. This sanding stick is made from a paint stirrer covered with sandpaper.

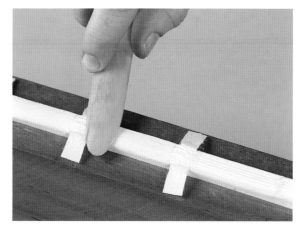

8. With the book secured in a finishing press, I apply muslin lining to the spine between the sewing stations but not over the tapes. I rub each lined section with a bone folder.

9. After all the linings are on, the book is removed from the press and placed between the temporary boards to dry. Once dry, I can fray the ends of the tapes.

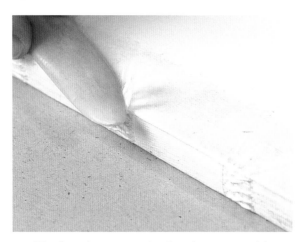

10. The frayed tapes are glued to the waste endsheet.

11. Endbands are made by rolling bookcloth or leather around a core. A piece of binder's board with notches helps secure the core while wrapping the cloth. After gluing, a bone folder rubs the cloth tight to the cord, and the endband is left to dry on the board.

12. Since the endbands only come to the middle of the first and last signatures, I measure them to this length, then cut them accordingly. Using PVA that has been brushed away from the book, I attach the endbands at the head of the book. I repeat this for the tail.

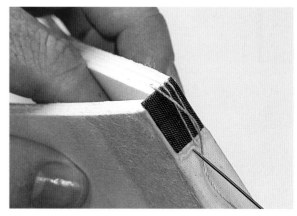

13. When the glue is dry, the endbands are over-stitched with silk or linen thread to further secure them and to add a decorative element.

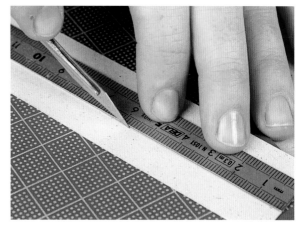

14. A piece of flexible card stock will become the spine liner. It needs to be cut grain long to the size of the spine. A sharp scalpel cuts a slight bevel on the spine liner's long edges.

15. After a piece of bookcloth is cut 1 inch (2.5 cm) larger than the spine liner in height and width, the spine liner is glued up and centered on the cloth. I use a 50/50 glue mix for turning in the head and tail.

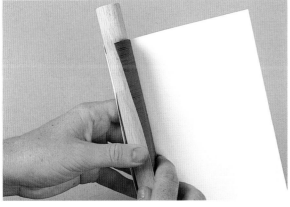

16. I like to wrap the spine piece around a dowel to dry—this encourages it to keep a rounded shape that is close to the shape of the spine.

17. While waiting for the spine piece to dry, a ¼-inch (.6 cm) strip from the head and tail of the waste endsheets is removed to ensure that no paper will extend beyond the height of the endsheets.

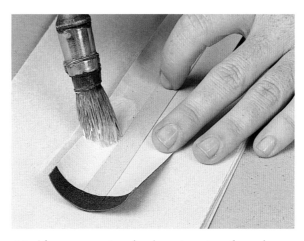

18. After unwrapping the dry spine piece from the dowel, I apply glue to either side of the lining but not on the area of lining paper that will curve around the spine.

19. Once the spine piece is positioned on the book, I first pinch it into place at the middle. Then working toward the ends, I push the spine piece tight to the book's spine.

20. Covers are cut from binder's board to the same height as the spine piece and to the exact width of the book block. I bevel and sand the spine edge and mark the boards for their final cut. After cutting the fore-edge (not the bevel!) they are covered with paper or cloth. A ½-inch (1.3 cm) turn-in width is used for the average book.

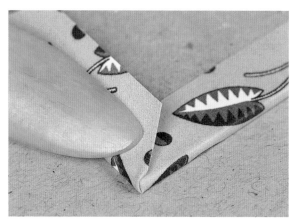

21. The corners are mitered, which leaves one-and-a-half board thicknesses of covering material to cover the corner.

22. Using 100% PVA, I brush it all the way out to the edge along the inside beveled edge of the board.

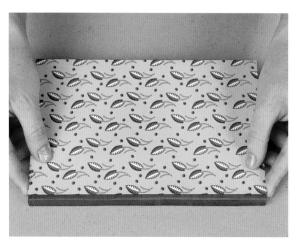

23. After placing the board on the book to determine its position, it's pressed down to anchor the cover.

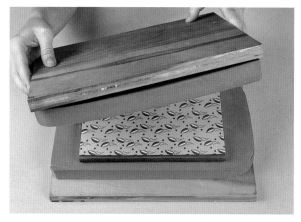

24. The book is carefully placed between pressing boards lined with thick, dense foam or a folded towel. I like using a smooth, uncoated kneeling pad made for gardening.

25. The book and boards are placed in a nipping press with a good bit of pressure—this ensures that the cover will be completely and uniformly attached. After a few minutes in the press, the book is removed and I repeat this procedure for the other cover. Once the book is back in the press, it's left to dry overnight.

26. Any loose part of the waste end sheet that's not glued down is torn out. Tearing it gently toward the gutter of the book prevents an excessive amount of board from pulling up with the paper.

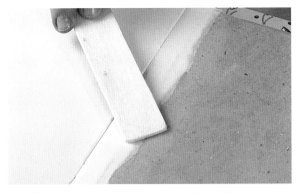

27. To eliminate any lumps or step down from the spine piece to the board, a sanding stick sands this transition area smooth.

28. In order to make the inside of the cover as smooth as possible, I line the remaining uncovered area of the board with a text-weight paper.

29. Endsheet paper, cut to the same height as the text block and twice the width, is folded in half and tipped in place, then glued using a 50/50 mixture along the gutter edge of the outer pages. The waste paper will protect the outer pages when gluing and will absorb any excess moisture.

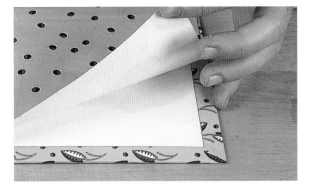

30. After gluing the last endsheet, I remove the waste paper and close the book, opening it carefully to rub it down. Absorbent paper goes between the text block and covers, before the book is weighted to dry overnight.

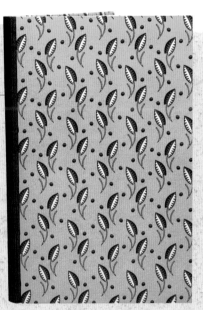

About the Artist

EILEEN WALLACE holds an M.F.A. in Book Arts and an M.L.S., both from the University of Alabama. She currently teaches Artist's Books at Columbus College of Art and Design in Columbus, OH. She recently spent three semesters teaching Book Arts and Papermaking for the University of Georgia's Studies Abroad program in Cortona, Italy. Since 1996, she has been a co-director of the Paper and Book Intensive.

From 1994 to 1998, Eileen was the studio coordinator for the Books, Paper and Letterpress studios at Penland School of Crafts, and also served as a graphic designer for many of the school's publications. Her favorite activity was to print letterpress invitations and announcements on the Heidelberg KSBA. In 1999, Eileen returned to Penland as a resident artist in bookbinding.

She teaches frequent workshops across the country and maintains a private studio producing books and boxes. In 2003, under her imprint Mile Wide Press, she began production on a line of printed decorative papers for books and related products. She exhibited in "The Nature of Craft and the Penland Experience" in celebration of Penland's 75th anniversary at The Mint Museum of Craft and Design in Charlotte, NC.

Gallery

My hope is that the artists represented here will illustrate the variety of media and materials from which I derive inspiration. I have long admired Hoss Haley's ability to distill everyday observations into iconic images of place—the economy of line and form establishing a delicate strength in his sculpture and drawings. His use of color and surface treatments on concrete and steel is reflected in Patch.

The paintings by Squeak Carnwath parallel my own interests in counting, observing, and keeping track of our daily lives. By incorporating words and dialogue with simple forms, she creates a visual narrative that is uniquely personal yet universally shared, suggesting the need to recognize beauty and importance in the simplicity of life.

For unmatched bookbinding technique, Mick LeTourneaux's books achieve a level of exactitude to which we all aspire. His strong and flexible bindings demonstrate technical precision and innovative adaptations of traditional methods while creating visual interest through exposed sewing and bold lacing patterns.

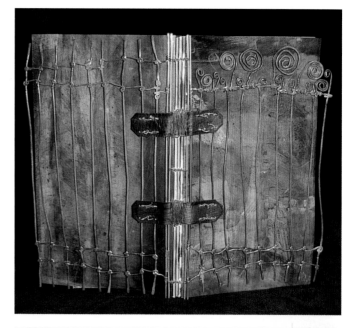

Laura Wait, *Garden Gateway,* 1999. 5¼ x 10¼ x 1¼ inches (13 x 25.6 x 3.1cm). Copper wire cover; text is painted paper and mylar with acrylic and paste medium; colored pencils. *Photos by the artist.*

Laura Wait's books represent the successful combination of personal expression with solid bookbinding skills. She effortlessly moves into the realm of artist's books in Cross, which is skillfully bound and illustrated through the use of strong color and commanding images. Alas, this is just a small sampling of the works too numerous to include by these and so many other talented artists.

Hoss Haley, *Patch,* 2002. 18 x 26 x 4 inches
(45 x 65 x 10 cm). Paint on steel. *Photo by Ken Pitts.*

Laura Wait, *Cross,* 2003. 5¾ x 9 x ⅝ inches (14.4 x 22.5 x 1.6 cm). Hand-painted pages with multi media paint on top of original
etchings by the artist; some hand-stamped text, goatskin spine, painted wood boards. *Photo by the artist.*

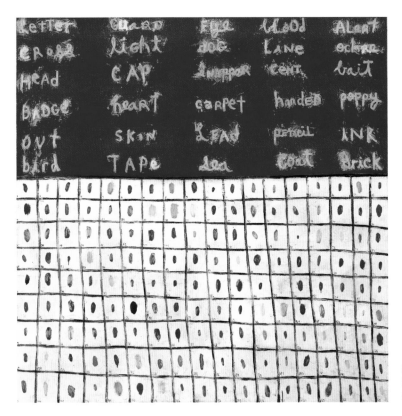

Squeak Carnwath, *What is Red,* 1994. 80 x 80 inches (200 x 200 cm). Oil and alkyd on canvas.
Photo by M. Lee Fatherree.

Squeak Carnwath, *Precious Ocean,* 1995. 48 x 48 inches (120 x 120 cm). Oil and alkyd on canvas.
Photo by M. Lee Fatherree.

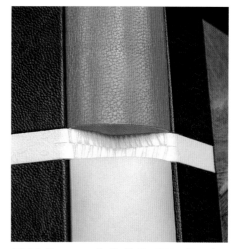

Mick LeTourneaux, *Saddle Binding,* 2002. 13¼ x 10½ x 1⅝ inches (33 x 26 x 4 cm). Text block sewn on split alum-tawed thongs; paste paper boards with leather spine edge; saddle spine construction made up of leather and vellum panels; rolled leather headbands. *Photo by the artist.*

Mick LeTourneaux, *Limp-Vellum Variation,* 2002. 6⅓ x 6¾ x 2⅖ inches (15.8 x 16. 8 x 6 cm). Text block sewn long-stitch on pigskin tongs; tanned pigskin spine piece; paper board pieces; full text block paper bonnet serves as anchor for non-adhesive structure. *Photo by the artist.*

Diseño • Desi

Derramo una capa de sal sobre la mes
y trazo un círculo con mi dedo.
Este es el ciclo de la vida
le digo a nadie.
Esta es la rueda de la fortuna,
el Círculo Artico.
Este es el anillo de Kerry
y la rosa blanca de Tralee
les digo a los fantasmas de mi famili
los padres muertos,
la tía que se ahogó,
mis hermanos y hermanas venideros,
mis hijos por nacer.
Este es el sol con sus rayos reluciente
y la luna amarga.
Este es el círculo absoluto de la geom
le digo a la hendidura en la pared,
a los pájaros xue cruzan por la venta
Esta es la rueda xue acabo de inventa
para rodar por el resto de mi vida
lo digo
tocando mi lengua con el dedo.

Versión de Miguel Angel Zapata

Diseno/Design, a broadside poem by Billy Collins, 2003. Translated into Spanish by Miguel-Angel Zapata. Illustrated with a linoleum cut by Carlos Ayress Moreno. 14 x 20 inches (35.6 x 50.8 cm). Designed and printed on Mohawk Superfine Cover by Steve Miller and students, Parallel Editions. Edition of 100 copies signed by the author. *Photo by Teresa Golson.*

lly Collins

pour a coating of salt on the table
nd make a circle in it with my finger.
his is the cycle of life
say to no one.
say to no one.
his is the wheel of fortune,
e Arctic Circle.
his is the ring of Kerry
nd the white rose of Tralee
say to the ghosts of my family,
e dead fathers,
e aunt who drowned,
y unborn brothers and sisters,
y unborn children.
his is the sun with its glittering spokes
nd the bitter moon.
his is the absolute circle of geometry
say to the crack in the wall,
the birds who cross the window.
his is the wheel I just invented
o roll through the rest of my life
say
ouching my finger to my tongue.

Steve Miller

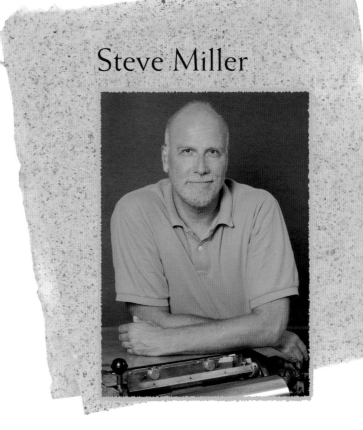

Steve Miller's books and broadsides
present the reader with an interplay
of text, image, and color set in
subtle compositional drama. His
works create a powerful testament to
the marriage of imagery and word.
In demonstrating the reduction
linoleum cut, he presents one low-
tech approach to introducing image.

Introducing the Image

By His Own Labor: The Biography of Dard Hunter, Cathleen A. Baker, 2000. 7¾ x 11¼ inches (19.4 x 28.1 cm). Front piece is a two-block wood engraving by John DePol; handmade paper from Twinrocker Mill; special endsheets made for the edition by Dard Hunter III from his grandfather's watermarked mould and deckle. Box by Judi Conant. Printed by Steve Miller, with printer's devil Cathleen A. Baker, at Red Hydra Press. Full leather binding by Grey Parrot. *Photo by Teresa Golson.*

In 1975, I simply needed to make a book of my own poems and wanted to learn letterpress printing to do so. I was living in Madison, Wisconsin, when Walter Hamady of the Perishable Press agreed to take me on as a guest student in his printing class at the university. Taking the first proof of a poem set in metal type, on paper I made out of blue jeans, was like being struck by lightning. Letterpress was everything I was passionate about—art, craft, literature, design, color, landscape, and books—all rolled into one fascinating challenge.

After finishing my own book in 1976, I began printing and binding limited editions of 100 to 200 copies of new works by poets and fiction writers I loved. My second book was a poetry chapbook by Diane Wakoski, *George Washington's Camp Cups,* and the sale of it bought my first printing press. I set up shop in an old welfare hotel near the railroad tracks in Madison, Wisconsin, where for three years I made numerous books and broadsides. The call of larger challenges and more direct contact with authors and artists led me to load a big white milk truck with all my worldly possessions and printing equipment, and move to a loft near the World Trade Center in New York City. I was joined there by Ken Botnick, who became a full partner at Red Ozier Press.

For the next nine years we made book after book, filled with poems, stories, and artwork. In 1988, a wonderful opportunity arose for going to the University of Alabama to teach what I loved doing. So I moved on, and Red Ozier Press ended. My imprint now is Red Hydra Press, and I make books when I can, between bouts of teaching and university duties.

I first heard of the reduction linoleum cut while studying the works of Pablo Picasso. I loved the boldness of cutting the block and printing, then recutting into the unknown, burning bridges while editioning color after color. At the end there was either success or failure—a print that was very exciting, or one that didn't quite hit the mark. I have created both over the course of making many of these.

Not to scare you away, but the reduction linoleum cut, or reduction linocut as it's known, is a devil. It appears simple: cutting away more of the block after each press run. But the process is hard to grasp and is fraught with the possibility for mistakes. It's like standing at the edge of a cliff not knowing exactly what will happen next. There's a reason it is sometimes called the "suicide block." For the person who needs solid ground to stand on and a clear path forward, this process can be harrowing. For the risk taker, it's a satisfying gamble. But anyone who tries it knows that at the end of the process, when the block is reduced to all but a few marks, some kind of victory over predictability has been won, and you realize it was fun.

Since my work involves making multiples—editioning art and type—that closely resemble each other, I decided to use the Vandercook proof press for demonstrating a reduction linocut in my Hands On section. While it's what I use, I realize not every person has access to a printing press, and for that reason I will also show how this same process can be done by hand. Fortunately for the book artist today, there are many letterpress studios and opportunities to learn how to print. If you are interested in finding out more about letterpress printing you may want to explore such places as Penland School of Crafts, the Minneapolis Center for Book Arts, the Center for Book Arts in New York City, Oregon College of Art and Craft in Portland, and the San Francisco Center for the Book. In addition, you may find a letterpress printer or hobbyist in your own town.

Many people from a variety of perspectives find the technology of letterpress fascinating and mysterious. Letterpress printing enjoys a strong following among individuals who want to make books by hand. These people are writers, artists, enthusiasts of the craft and tools of printing, and historians of the book and the technology of book making. Thrown into the

Bostrophedon, 2000. 16 x 16 inches (40 x 40 cm) folded down to 4 x 4 inches (10 x 10 cm). Mixed media; a collaboration with three students, employing photopolymer printing plates and type. Printed by Steve Miller and students. *Photo by Teresa Golson.*

JANET KAUFFMAN

On Eliminating Characters
from Fiction

If you don't say the name of a person, a good
many things are possible in a sentence, and even
in a landscape without margins or verifiable
boundaries. It is possible to turn a corner and
encounter a large machine lifting trees out of the
ground. You can read the lettering on the metal,
letters and numbers that are a code name for the
machine, but it is certainly not the name of a
person. Heaps of trees in full leaf may be stacked
in the middle of the road. It is possible to see the
beginnings of flames among the branches, and
if you wait long enough, not very long, turn
slightly to the side, and still not saying the name
of a person, you can walk through the fire and
into the house it's become.

UA Bankhead Visiting Writers Series 1.25.2001 | S. Miller • P. Moxon

My Twelve Steps

You can't ask me to keep you alive.
You can't expect me to be your only friend.
You can't make me be both parents.
You can't force me to be your watchdog.
You can't keep me from my friends.
You can't tell me all those lies.
You can't ask me to forgive you.
You can't expect me to keep you sober.
You can't force me to be so alone.
You can't make me your adversary.
You can't keep secrets from me.
You can't tell me that you are sorry.

Emily Martin, 1996

Two Poems, Janet Kauffman and Emily Martin, 2001. 5 ½ x 10¾ inches (13.8 x 27 cm). Illustrations by Steve Miller and Paul Moxon. Reduction linocut; photopolymer printing plates, type. Printed by Miller and Moxon.
Photo by Teresa Golson.

mix are those interested in antiques as well as those who make bric-a-brac frames for their living room walls from type-storage cases, known as California job cases.

In the 1960s, when letterpress technology was being suddenly and furiously replaced by photolithography and computer-set type, small-press publishers and artists discovered that wonderful proof presses and California job cases of used type were being hauled to the dump. For very little money, and sometimes just for the taking, the type and presses were appropriated for a new mission—printing limited edition books and broadsides of literature and art, which are printed on one side of a piece of paper and are suitable for framing.

The mimeograph machine no longer satisfied since the letterpress allowed a greater deal of control for making printed pieces. The small publisher could take the means of production completely in hand—from the carefully selected manuscript, all the way through to the stacked piles of books ready for friends or the marketplace. When first learning to make books by hand on a press, traditional rules and forms were often followed, but quickly the excitement of unlimited possibilities reared its head, and artist's books were born.

People come to letterpress from various worlds. One approach is exacting and attempts to perfect the kiss of metal type and printing plates to paper. It is an attempt to reproduce the best of how books have been printed by hand. The first time I saw a *Gutenberg Bible* in the Rare Book Room of the New York Public Library, I was astounded by how perfectly it was printed. Just the right amount of very black ink on the face of the metal types struck the handmade paper with just the right amount of impression, or bonk. Letterpress printing has not been better executed than in its earliest manifestation. There are many who attempt to print as well as the very first printers, and they sometimes succeed.

On the other hand there are people who see letterpress equipment as an opportunity for wild artistic expression. They know that liberties can be taken with the medium, and they push the envelope. For these hardy folks, old presses are one more tool in an arsenal available to make books, printed pieces, and printed objects. Often the newcomers have just enough information and training to make them dangerous in a letterpress studio, and I've seen many beautiful experimental projects.

I approach letterpress somewhere in the middle. I shoot for perfection but know that making conces-

Untitled Broadside, 2002. 6 x 16 inches (15 x 40 cm). Mixed media including Sandragraph and found images; words, illustration, and printing by Red Hydra Press.
Photo by Teresa Golson

sions is sometimes essential to moving ahead. I will do battle with the press in an attempt to print perfectly on any given day, but I also understand surrender after working out a strategic compromise. When I teach letter-press, it is in the spirit of exciting beginners to the many possibilities that letterpress presents—the challenges, the limitations, the standards of what is acceptable for inking and impression. But above all, I strive to introduce them to the joy of making a project from the very first glimmer of an idea to the finished books stacked in a neat pile.

The older I get, the more interesting I find it to break rules. Not rules of quality, because bad inking is always bad inking, and bad habits in preparation or at press are bad habits that I will stomp out if at all possible. But the aesthetic and artistic rules and mandates I learned no longer have such a strong sway over me. One of these rules goes to the heart of how I introduce letterpress to students.

I was taught that type and printed images are most appropriate side-by-side—that over-lapping or layering type and image was a cardinal sin. People who make artist's books often make a great potpourri of text and image, but to me everything ends up all looking the same after awhile. Colors and words spread all over the pages compete page after page for attention. But a judicious interplay of text and image, the careful play of color, subtle compositional drama, and layers of meaning can be very exciting. When my students create images to be printed using letterpress technology, the challenge I present is to associate imagery with words.

In the studio, we first make the simplest of printing plates. These are low-relief plates made from a piece of ¾-inch (1.9 cm) plywood brushed over with acrylic gel medium, covered with muslin cloth, then brushed and combed again with gel medium on top of the muslin. When printed, the dried gel medium shows the slightest marks made on it. When the plate dries it is put in the bed of the press,

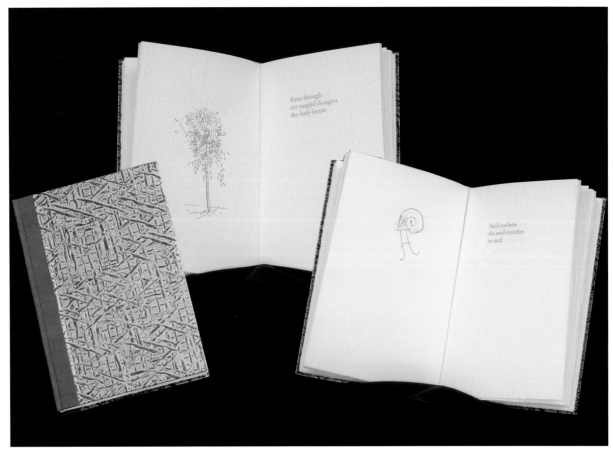

inked up, and printed. Harry and Sandra Reese of Turkey Press popularized this kind of low-relief plate making, calling it a "Sandragraph." It is often employed as a subtle background to words and art printed and layered over it.

These plates are experimental and unpredictable— you hardly ever know what you are going to get— and that's the lovely part of it. Things may be embedded under the muslin like leaves and string (or like the thin rubber gloves a Penland student once glued between muslin and plywood—the gel medium never really dried and the gloves would ooze every time the press' cylinder passed over it—not a pretty sight!). By adding some type—a quote, a poem, or something from the printer's journal evoked by the atmosphere set up within the print—imagery and words combine to create a powerful statement.

As I present each new technique to students, I like to up the ante. And that's where the reduction linocut comes in. The process of cutting into linoleum to make a printing surface is fairly straightforward. Linoleum is not a difficult medium with which to work. Linoleum cutting tools are inexpensive and

readily available at art and hobby stores. They come with a number of interchangeable cutting ends used for creating different kinds of shaped cuts. Linoleum may be found in rolls or flat sheets, which may then be cut and printed by hand or with an etching press, as well as mounted on a wood block and printed by hand or in a printing press. I recommend using linoleum mounted on a block.

There are many sources for drawings that can be made into linoleum cuts. A simple drawing can be sketched, or a tracing made from a more complex drawing or photograph. I once made a drawing from a photo of a tornado I pulled off a website. Linoleum is a fairly crude medium, so the drawing you wish to transfer must be simple. Thin lines do not survive, broad strokes do. Tiny details get lost. When you create a reduction print, think of simple forms layering over simple forms. Reducing a complicated scene to its essential shapes is an exciting challenge. I like to work in pencil, because I can erase and redraw along the way. I use tracing paper so I can see through it to the image I am simplifying.

I work with a good pair of scissors, tracing paper,

sharp pencils, carbon paper, a ruler, and a palette knife for distributing ink on a piece of glass or marble so it can be evenly picked up by the brayer. I use a good brayer that is approximately 4 inches (10 cm) long. People who carve in linoleum often purchase or make a bench hook. It hooks to the edge of a table and braces the block while cutting, since it's very easy to cut yourself badly on the sharp tool if the block or your fingers slip. I often have a small block on hand to experiment with before cutting into the block I'll be using for my print. I'd recommend your first lino blocks be on the small side. The larger the block, the more gouging away of vast areas of linoleum you will face.

For ink, I use rubber or oil-based letterpress inks, though I also use water-based inks. The effects are different, and it's worth experimenting with both. Water-based inks need to be slathered on, while letterpress inks make it easier to create thinner layers of ink; thin layers work better when printing multiple layers. One principle remains true with reduction prints: it is hard to see a light color printed over a darker one. Therefore, the first color to be printed must be a light or pale one, the second run a medium color, and the third still darker.

I use newsprint cut to the final size of the print for taking proofs of the block. Once the inking is right, the block cut or corrected just the way I want it, and I've found the place on the piece of paper where the image will be printed, I will print a half dozen "position" proofs to use for alignment purposes on subsequent runs.

I describe linoleum as a flexible medium open to interpretation. What I mean is that how crudely or perfectly you cut the linoleum, how much ink you decide to apply, how much pressure you deploy when you print—all of these and more have an impact on how the final print appears. Will it be printed with very little ink and pressure to suggest an image, or will the colors be solid and even? How much in the way of atmospheric vagrant cutting marks will you leave or cut away? Sometimes proofs show that extraneous linoleum will need to be cut away so that only the drawing prints. However, the cutting marks and the patterns it creates can be interesting and can become a dynamic part of the composition.

An Alabama Kozo Primer, account by Glenn House, 1995. 7 x 11 inches (17.5 x 27.5 cm). Illustrated by Richard Flavin. Alabama kozo hand-made paper sample included. The binding wrapper utilizes a Japanese Momi-gami process. Printed by Steve Miller and students, Parallel Editions, The University of Alabama.
Photo by Teresa Golson

The Search For A True History of Alabama, Howell Raines, 1994. 5¾ x 9¼ inches (23 x 12.8 cm). Illustrated by Christopher McAfee; calligraphy by Glen Epstein. Printed and bound by Steve Miller at Red Hydra Press. *Photo by Teresa Golson.*

These are decisions that you as the creator will make, and there is no correct answer. There is room for many looks in this medium. It's up to you. I like to play with all the options when I am "making ready"— getting the block properly positioned and inked and ready to print. I used to pound the heck out of a block and use lots of ink. I'd pass over the block several times or more between each print to cover it heavily and evenly. That doesn't appeal to me any longer. I'm more interested in translucency, and actually seeing some of the grain of the linoleum in the print.

Oh, and did I tell you this process is really fun? The fact is, despite its challenge, the printed pieces are always interesting. People who don't think of themselves as artists are always shocked that the process yields something that is often quite beautiful.

The Chinese Painting

Through the pink slit of dawn, they arrive
filling the bedroom with cool whistles—

down-drenched swans and their wet
voices—ribbons in the rain.

Night's blurred line skims the lake,
its surface a pearled luster.

Their wide wings arc—
each call, an urgency.

Night is dwindling, I hear one say
as the sky empties.

Mary Wehner

Drawing by Jane Marshall
Seventy-five letterpress-printed copies by Steve Miller
Red Hydra Press, Tuscaloosa, 2003

The Chinese Painting, broadside, poem by Mary Wehner, 2003. 8½ x 15 inches (21.3 x 37.5 cm). Illustrated by Jane Marshall. Printed on dampened Nideggen mouldmade paper by Steve Miller at Red Hydra Press. *Photo by Teresa Golson.*

Hands On

Steve demonstrates making a reduction linoleum cut, where each successive cut on the block reduces it while adding another layer to the print. He shows how to transfer the design to the block and how to cut it, then shows how to take the proof on the letterpress and print the sheets. He also demonstrates how to print a block by hand.

The Reduction Linocut for the Press

1. The tools and materials for creating a linocut

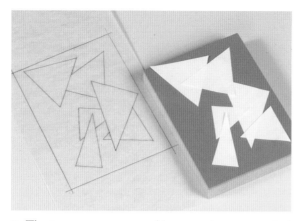

2. The image was composed by arranging geometrical shapes of cut-out paper on the linoleum block. Once I was satisfied with the design, I laid tracing paper over it and pencilled in the shapes as well as the corners and edges of the block.

3. The tracing-paper drawing is cleaned up and the shapes marked as to which will be cut away first, second, and third for a three-color print. Numbering is important since anything you cut away from the block will appear as the color of the paper.

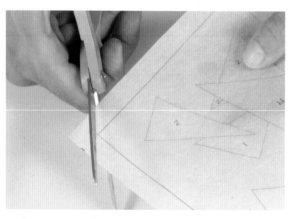

4. Scissors trim the tracing paper, leaving a ½-inch (1.3 cm) border around the penciled edge of the block. Then the corners are cut away.

5. The drawing is placed face down on the block and the edge of the tracing paper is folded over the side. This will transfer the drawing in reverse on the block, then, when printed, the drawing will reverse and appear as a positive on the page.

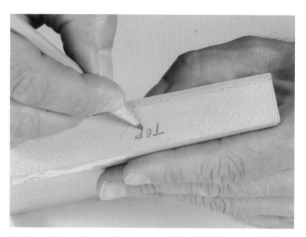

6. In order to keep things in order, TOP is marked both at the top of the tracing paper and on the top of the lino block.

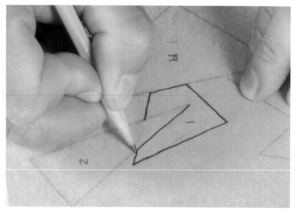

7. A sharp pencil traces over the drawing, transferring it to the block. Since traces of pencil, ink, or carbon-paper (see step 9) that are left on the block will print for a few runs when taken to press, it's best to transfer only the parts of the drawing that will be needed for that particular cutting.

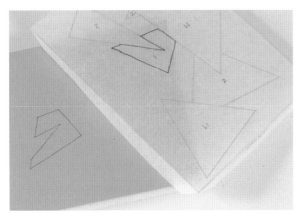

8. The first part of the drawing transferred to the block

9. Using carbon paper is an alternate way of getting the drawing on the block. A piece of carbon paper is laid on the linoleum and the tracing-paper jig laid on top of it.

10. Afterward, a pencil traces the image from the tracing-paper jig, transferring it to the block.

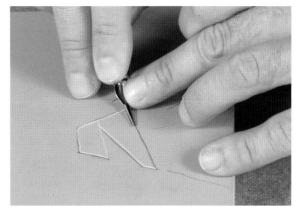

11. With the block secured on a bench hook, a fine-line cutting tool first outlines the shape. A V-gouge is then used to take more material away from the edge of the outline.

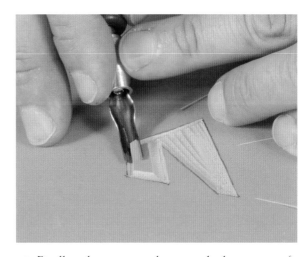

12. Finally, a large gouge clears out the large areas of linoleum inside the shape. Because the printing press applies a fair amount of pressure between block and paper, it's necessary to cut away a lot of the linoleum away or it will print as vagrant marks.

13. I lock the block with its first cut in the bed of the press.

14. The Vandercook is inked with the lightest of the three colors that will be used.

15. A proof of the linocut is taken. It's important to take plenty of position proofs.

16. The proof shows that additional packing is needed to achieve the proper pressure for printing. Packing is made from sheets of paper that are placed under the block.

17. Here the printed sheets are laid out for drying. (Only printers get to see the sheets laid out in all their glory.) After each print, I clean the block.

18. Here I'm tracing the second set of lines onto the cleaned block.

19. A pencil corrects the transferred line on the block.

20. An X marks the parts of the block that need to be cut away.

21. The block is cut away for the second time.

22. The second color is printed over the first (dried) color, adding depth to the emerging print.

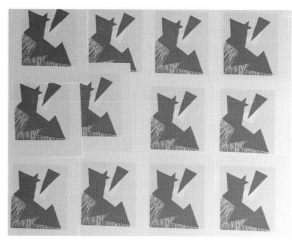

23. The second-run sheets are laid out to dry.

24. This is the final cut. Notice that most of the linoleum has been cut away by the previous cuts.

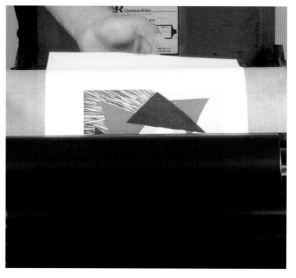

25. The third color is printed, revealing the final image.

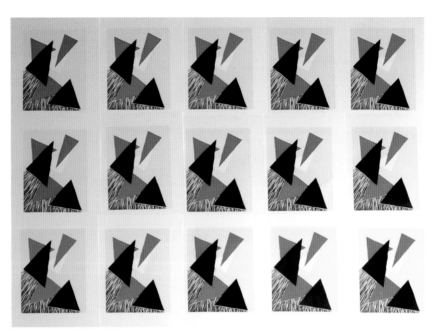

26. The editioned prints are laid out side-by-side on a table to dry.

Printing a Linocut by Hand

27. Using a pallet knife, I spread ink on glass.

29. Then the brayer inks the linocut.

28. The proper way to ink a brayer is by rolling the brayer in the ink on the glass.

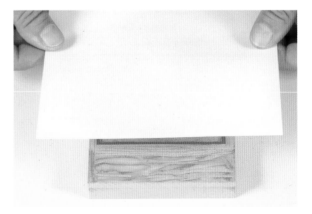

30. You must register the paper on the linocut for printing.

31. Applying pressure by hand positions the paper on the linocut.

32. A clean brayer is used to transfer the ink to the paper.

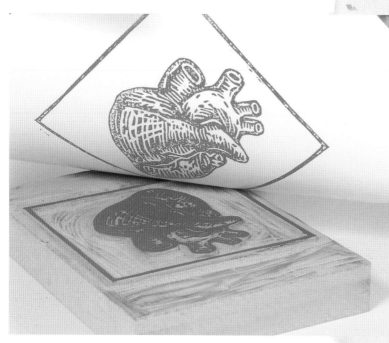

33. Pulling the finished print off the block.

About the Artist

In 1976 STEVE MILLER founded Red Ozier Press in Madison, WI, devoted to publishing literary, hand-made, limited first editions. In 1979, Miller moved the press to New York City, where, with Ken Botnick, it achieved national prominence.

The New York Public Library purchased the entire archive of Red Ozier Press for its permanent collection in 1988, including all proofs and correspondence from over 60 publications. In October of 1993, the Humanities Gallery at Cooper Union in New York City was the site of a month-long retrospective exhibition of the work of the press, which coincided with the publication of *The Red Ozier: A Literary Fine Press, 1976–1987*, by Michael Peich, co-published by The New York Public Library and Yellow Barn Press.

Miller began his career at the University of Alabama in 1988 as an associate professor in the School of Library and Information Studies. He teaches letterpress printing and hand papermaking in the graduate Book Arts Program.

Miller is the proprietor of Red Hydra Press. In January of 2003, he produced a poem broadside, *The Names*, by U.S. Poet Laureate Billy Collins, with a Sandragraph plate by Miller.

Miller is a co-director of the Paper and Book Intensive, a nationally recognized annual series of summer workshops in the book arts. He is chair of the advisory board of the American Museum of Papermaking in Atlanta, GA, and is past president of the Friends of Dard Hunter, Inc. He is a recipient of grants from the New York State Council on the Arts and the National Endowment for the Arts.

Gallery

*T*he book artists in my gallery have experience and longevity, as well as sparkling new talent. I use the term "book artist" cautiously, for the term is sometimes used with abandon. What I mean is someone who is absolutely committed to the book as a vehicle for deep meaning. Too often people come to making their book ill-prepared for the mechanical aspects of production and use the book form as a platform for highly personal self-expression. The value of this can be debated, but I think a book is best when conceptually larger than the person making it.

In addition to their passion for the book itself, the persons in my gallery also share a passion for teaching others about bookmaking. Handmade books are mysterious and unfathomable to most people. People assume books appear out of the ether on bookshelves. I have seen the look of disbelief when talking to people about how books are made by hand. Unbelievable—you make books? If you want to find your way in the world of creating books by hand you are obliged to teach others to value the handmade book, and these people do.

Inge Bruggeman and Katherine Ruffin represent the new generation of book artists: they have books in the hopper at all times, and balance their excellent art and craft with teaching. Both are fearless in getting out into the world. William Drendel and Bonnie Stahlecker are well-regarded figures known to many, taught by many, and thoughtfully edgy in their thinking about alternative book forms. Harry Reese taught me and many others how to make wonderful "Sandragraph" low-relief printing plates to create background excitement on the page. He and wife Sandra run the is highly respected Turkey Press. I have never met Chris Stern but have admired the dramatic and inspired work from afar. All are good people who have, against the odds, made making books their lives.

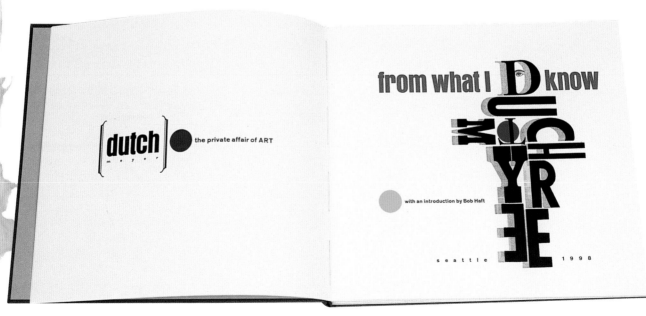

C. Christopher Stern, *From What I Know by Dutch Meyer,* 1998. 11 x 10 inches (27.5 x 25 cm). Letterpress printed using metal type and tipped in photos; hand bound. Deluxe boxed edition includes a unique art piece by Dutch Meyer inset into each box. *Photos by Greg Valazza and Mark Sullo.*

C. Christopher Stern, *From What I Know by Dutch Meyer.* Cover

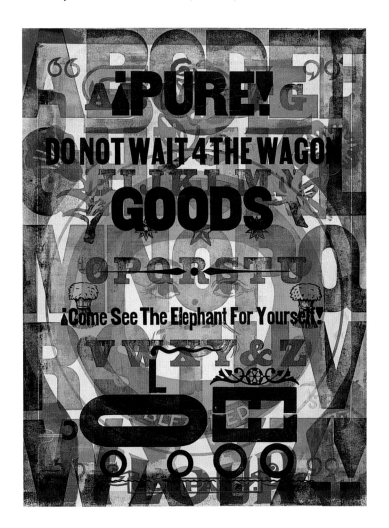

C. Christopher Stern, *Pure Goods,* 2001. 17½ x 23½ inches (43.8 x 58.8 cm). Letterpress relief print of wood and metal types, using 19th-century advertising cuts and slogans.
Photos by Mark Sullo.

Bonnie Stahlecker, *Directions for a Successful Life,* 1999-2000. 15½ x 2⅝ inches (38.8 x 6.6 cm). Somerset heavyweight text paper; relief, monoprint, and letterpress printed with the use of stencils; sewn on seven linen tapes slotted into boards covered with painted Moriki. *Photos by artist.*

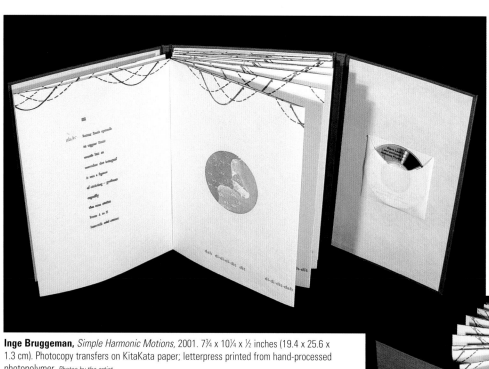

Inge Bruggeman, *Simple Harmonic Motions,* 2001. 7¾ x 10¼ x ½ inches (19.4 x 25.6 x 1.3 cm). Photocopy transfers on KitaKata paper; letterpress printed from hand-processed photopolymer. *Photos by the artist.*

William Drendel, *Saturday Noon—By the Time He Realized He Should Be Happy, It Was Too Late,* 1998. 7 x 7½ x 1¼ inches (17.5 x 18.8 x 3.1 cm). Shredded found book; Japanese paper-covered boards with crimped disc from climate control machine. *Photo by the artist.*

Harry Reese, Untitled (from *33⅓: Off the Record*), 1995.18 x 18 inches (45 x 45 cm). Monotype print; oil paint on Magnani Italia paper; printed on a Vandercook 219 press from a 33⅓ LP vinyl record. *Photo by the artist.*

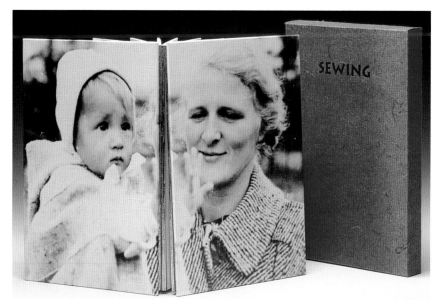

Katherine McCanless Ruffin, *Sewing,* 1995. 5 x 7½ inches (12.5 x 18.8 cm). Johannot paper, photolinen covered boards; hand-made paper slipcase; letterpress printed with photocopy transfer images of family photographs; hand binding. *Photos by Steve Gyurina.*

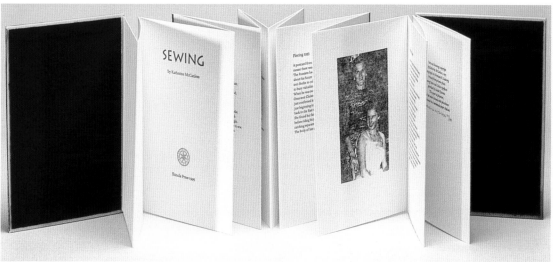

Carol Barton

The magic inherent in Carol Barton's pop-up structures is a source of delight and amazement. Though children come to mind when pop-up books are mentioned, adults are just as charmed to turn a page and have an image spring to life in three-dimensional form. For those who question how it's done, Carol demonstrates the engineering behind the form.

Instructions for Assembly, (1993).
11 x 8¼ inches
(27.5 x 20.6 cm).
Mohawk Poseidon paper; pop-up, off-set lithography.
Printed by Nexus Press, Atlanta, Ga.
Photos by the artist.

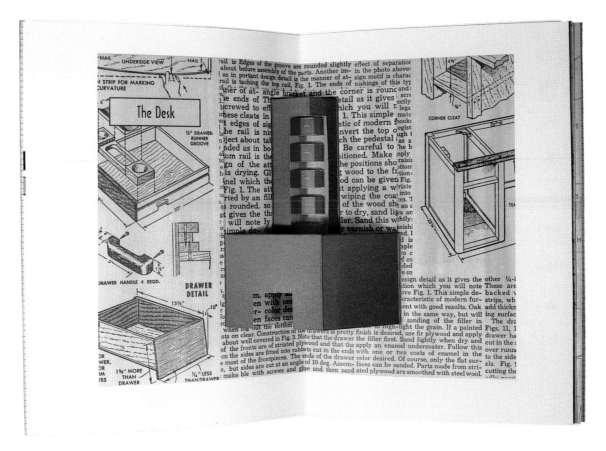

CAROL BARTON

Engineering the Magic

*Home Dreams,
1997 (also on
next page). 6 x 4
x 44 inches (15
x 10 x 110 cm).
Acrylic; laser-
print, accordion
book with hand-
cut pop-ups.
Photos by the artist.*

There's magic in a book that pops up! What's more, delight at this magic is not limited to the young reader. I have known serious, hardened academics to suddenly shed all traces of scholarly gravity as they gleefully recall a favorite childhood pop-up storybook. For the child, the magic is simply in seeing a dimensional form arise from the flat page. For the adult, there's the same initial surprise, but added to that is the mystery of how the piece actually works. Many are content to know that there are people in this world who have figured it out. But for others, solving the mystery is the real source of pleasure in the pop-up form.

A pop-up is not just a static paper sculpture. It moves with the turning of the page. In essence, the page is a mechanical lever and the pop-up is a little paper machine; it moves up to collapse within the closed book and drops down into its dimensional form when the page is opened. Designers of pop-ups thus are aptly titled paper engineers. It was this active element—the kinetic/mechanical/structural aspect—that first attracted me to explore the pop-up structure.

I've always enjoyed building things. I grew up building houses out of cardboard kitchen appliance boxes and geared whirligigs out of Tinker Toys. My father was a diesel engine mechanic, and I loved to play in his shop full of hand tools and scrap materials. Later, when I was in art school at Washington University in St. Louis, I had a sophomore design class that concentrated on dimensional and mechanical structures. The professor, Fern Tiger, was new to the school and reputed to be a stern taskmaster. She was. I learned a lot in the class—how to use shop tools, work with new materials, and, most importantly, how to solve functional design problems. Although I was a painting major, a lot of the groundwork for my later career as a sculptural bookmaker grew from these experiences.

Oddly enough, I don't recall any pop-up books from my childhood. My first encounter with the "book as sculpture" was when a friend showed me her rummage sale find, an Italian carousel book tracing the tale of Sleeping Beauty through multi-layered pages. Each page was composed of three layers of scenery, much like a stage set, with the characters posed within the scene. What captured my imagination was the amazing dimensionality of the images, and the fact that they collapsed into the flat structure of the book when it was closed.

At this point I had already created my first artist's book in an edition of 250 copies. After spending a year on the project, I had returned to painting as a career—bookmaking was too time-consuming and difficult. But seeing the Italian book changed my mind. I began to view the book as a place where my separate creative interests in narrative painting, photography, sculpture, and functional design could converge. I think the book's potential for this creative synthesis is what appeals to many artists. Intrigued by the pop-up form, I was off on a new career path.

Graduated and living in Washington, D.C., my paper engineering tutelage began in some of my favorite local hangouts: rare book libraries and museums. Lining the shelves of the Library of Congress, the Smithsonian Institution's Dibner Library, and the National Library of Medicine were troves of early movable and pop-up books that served as my guides. I learned that the earliest mechanical books, or "movables," dated back to the 14th century. In these, the viewer actively had to participate by turning a wheel or pulling a tab to activate the page. To my surprise, these early books were not meant for children, but were serious scientific treatises on such topics as astronomy, geometry, and human anatomy.

The true pop-up book did not appear until the early 19th century. Here the viewer simply turns the page and the pop-up springs up in all its dimensional brilliance. Most of these early pop-ups were produced for a young audience, but they undoubtedly delighted adults, too, and were avidly collected. By carefully examining how the pop-ups in such books were constructed (and sometimes peeking behind the pages to see the "guts" of the mechanisms), I began categorizing the various paper structures that would later serve me in my own work. Two of these structures, the V-fold and the asymmetrical pop-up, will be shown in

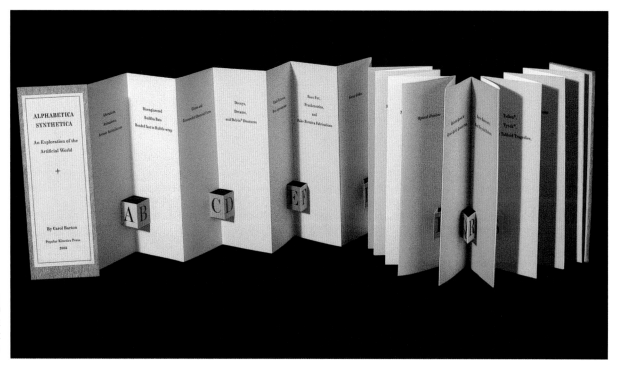

Alphabetica Synthetica,
2003. 7½ x 2½ x 70
inches (19 x 6.4 x
177.8 cm). Ink jet
printing. *Photo by the artist.*

the Hands On section. Both of these structures are very strong and can be adapted to a variety of visual images. They can be used independently, or combined to create a more complex pop-up scene with lots of dimensional levels.

As with any art form, a technique alone does not define a successful piece. Once I understood the basic pop-up structures, the real challenge was to combine visual themes with the architecture of the page. In the commercial world, the paper engineer and the illustrator often are two very different people, each with her own creative language and skill. For me, my narrative painting and photography interests sided with the illustrator while the sculptor and mechanic sided with the engineer. The engineer approaches a project from a structural viewpoint, realizing the physical limits of what is and is not possible when mechanizing paper. The illustrator can envision the subject, the theme, but may not understand the physical limitations of the moving paper form. A minor tug-of-war can result, with the physics usually winning out over the imagery. It's much easier when both mindsets exist in one head, but even then it's hard to envision the two simultaneously.

So where do I start, with the image or the engineering? Each project is different. Sometimes I have an idea for a great theme, but it takes months, even

years, for the physical aspects of the project to evolve. My latest book, *Alphabetica Synthetica,* grew from an alphabetical list of synthetic materials I've been maintaining for more than three years. But it was only recently that I finalized the pop-up block structure for the letters and the color scheme that is integral to the finished design (see above photo). At other points I may accidentally discover an interesting twist on a pop-up structure or sculptural binding, and then I search for just the right idea to fit the form. This was the case with *Vision Shifts* (see photos on page 73), which began with my accidental discovery that a window floating in a pop-up panel moves or shifts position as the page is opened, thus panning over the picture behind the window. The entire book, with its theme of shifting points of view and how they change our view of the world around us, is based on this mechanical movement.

In either case, I work on each level of the thought process through a series of verbal and visual models and sketches. I may start with a list of brainstormed words or with a quick paper engineering test done with a scrap of paper. From there, the idea evolves through a set of increasingly complex mockups. By the end of the project I may have 30 or 40 of these mockups, several for each aspect of the project. I make models to test my visual sequences, models of

Vision Shifts, 1998. 9 x 4¾ inches (22.5 x 11.9 cm), closed. Mohawk superfine paper; offset lithography with die-cut sliding pop-up windows; edition of 500. *Photos by the artist.*

the book's binding, models and many more models of the pop-ups, and models of the text and the typography. So much for spontaneity! But if the project is successful, it often looks as if it sprang from a single, instantaneous flash of inspiration. And that's my goal, to marry form and function to the point where they appear perfectly logical, almost effortless, belying the multiple failures, mistakes, and false starts behind the finished piece.

The pop-up elements of my books pose additional challenges. Aside from the actual engineering, there's the issue of the ideal position for each pop-up page and how this relates to the viewer. Various pop-up structures work best with the book viewed from different positions; some are viewed best with the book held upright, others with the book fully opened and flat on a table, still others with the page turned sideways at a 90° angle. Viewers usually are not aware of these differences, but if they are forced to continuously turn the book upside down and backwards to read it, they can be frustrated or, even worse, end up with a migraine. To prevent such disasters, I always try to create a pleasing rhythm in the sequencing of my pop-up pages. That's not to say that every page must be viewed from the same angle, but there should be an ease of flow to the turning of the page. Viewers

may remain unaware of these efforts to facilitate their visual comfort, but like most good design, successful innovations are often the least noticed because they seem so naturally logical.

Another consideration for me is the fact that I produce most of my artist's books in relatively large editions. Constructing pop-ups is labor intensive. Although the process of cutting them out has been mechanized, their assembly is still a hand process, even in the commercial world. Most commercial pop-up books are assembled in countries where labor costs are minimal, but I am my own assembly line and must think about the hours of time I'm willing to invest in putting my projects together.

I actually enjoy the assembly process. It's one in which my hands are busy, and my mind is free to wander and contemplate the next project or any number of intellectual challenges. In our modern, rush-rush society we have mechanized many of the traditionally repetitive daily tasks once required of our citizens, such as housecleaning and farm chores—usually to our gain. But I believe we need to retain some of this repetitive ritual to give rhythm to our lives and to relieve its stresses. I find my own meditative ritual in the repeated tasks of folding, cutting, and gluing required by my bookmaking. Additionally, I find the

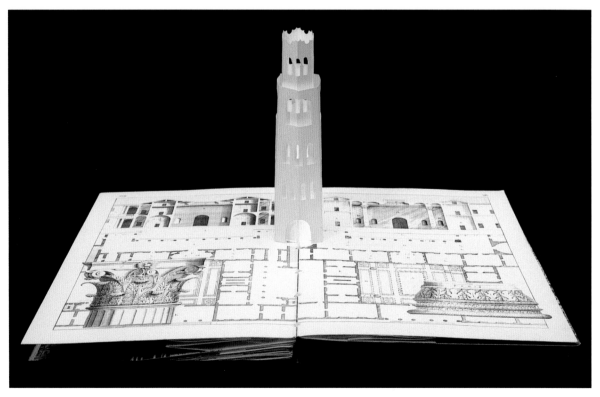

Five Luminous Towers, 2002. (28.8 x 19.4 x 7.5 cm). Mohawk superfine paper, light bulbs, batteries, fiber optic filament; offset lithography on laser-cut pop ups; edition of 50. *Photo by the artist.*

CAROL BARTON

job of streamlining production to be as creatively challenging as that of designing the original book. It's actually a process of redesign.

After the book has evolved through its many mockup stages to become an integrated piece, I rethink the entire project in terms of production. I tear the book apart and put it back together so that it requires the least amount of handwork possible, and then I invent the jigs and templates which speed up its manufacture even further.

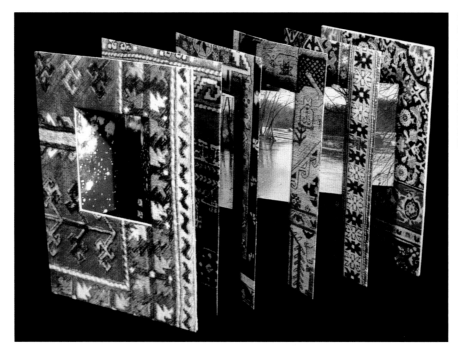

Loom, 1989. 5 x 7 x 9¾ inches (12.5 x 17.5 x 23.1 cm). Mohawk Superfine paper; offset lithography using press plates from graphite pencil drawings and photos; die-cut tunnel book; edition of 600. *Photo by the artist.*

I make jigs for positioning cover images onto book boards, for scoring and folding pop-ups, for gluing parts together in the correct order and position, and for cutting tabs and trimming edges. I design dies and patterns for cutting out the pop-up parts, and incorporate into these the score lines and folds that facilitate their assembly and cut down on the time required.

This brings me to the subject of die cutting and laser cutting. As I mentioned before, the process of cutting pop-ups has been mechanized. Die cutting uses a press to cut out paper shapes and press in score lines for folds. Large die cutting shops use specially designed, self-feeding presses for this procedure, but I use a letterpress—the type of press that employs cast lead type for printing text. To use a letterpress for die cutting, I remove the inking rollers and wrap a flexible steel jacket around the press cylinder, or insert a zinc plate over the bed of a clamshell press to protect it from the cutting blades of the die. I send a drawing of the cutting and scoring pattern to a die-maker in New York City, and a few weeks later I receive in the mail my made-to-order die. It looks like a cookie-cutter set

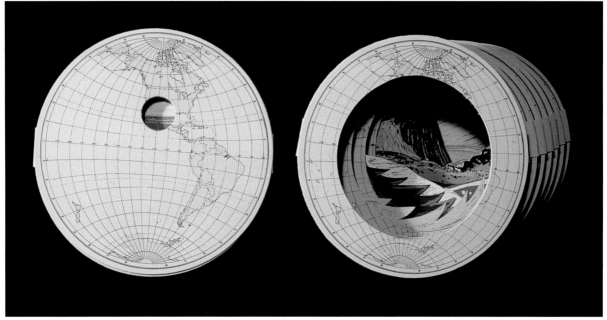

Tunnel Map, 1988. 9½ diameter x 10 inches (23.8 x 25 cm). Silkscreen; die-cut tunnel book; edition of 150. *Photo by the artist.*

Plant This Book, 1991. 5 x 3½ inches (12.5 x 8.8 cm). Mixed media, found seed packets; sewn binding on cords. *Photo by the artist.*

in plywood, with sharp blades for cutting and dull, rounded blades for scoring fold lines. I lock this die into my press in place of the lead type and hand feed the paper into the press. As the paper is pressed against the die, my pop-up parts are cut and scored.

A new technology for cutting very intricate pop-up parts uses a laser to literally burn through the paper. Laser cutting allows for an incredible amount of cut-

ting detail, but also requires access to what is currently an expensive piece of equipment. Moreover, cutting and scoring are two separate processes requiring different cutting depths. The pattern is taken directly from any vector-based computer drawing. I had my book *Five Luminous Towers* laser-cut because the small windows and details in the pop-up towers could not be die-cut. The results were astonishing. (See

The Pocket Paper Engineer, 2004. 4½ x 9½ inches (11.4 x 24 cm). An interactive how-to book with do-it-yourself pop-up models. *Photo by the artist.*

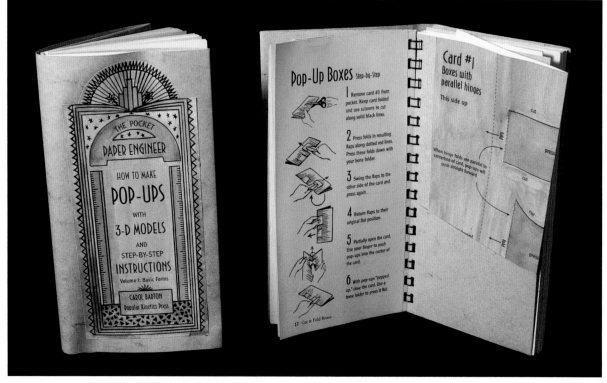

CAROL BARTON

page 74.) My dream is that the technology will soon become so affordable that every artist will be able to own her own personal laser cutter!

Of course, if you are making just a single book or a small edition, you will probably choose to do the cutting and scoring by hand. Die and laser cutting require a monetary investment in addition to printing or computer skills; for limited editions, old-fashioned manual labor may be the best route. Two of the most important design elements, aside from aesthetics, are time and money, and design is a constant balancing act between them. If you have lots of one, often you have little of the other, and you must choose when

you want to spend your money to have someone else do the job, and when you want to devote your own time to the project out of necessity, love of the work, or a personal need for control. Skill and the need for precision also may dictate when a job is done manually and when it is best done mechanically.

Why use a pop-up structure? Every choice in a book project—typography, materials, sequencing, and construction—either enhances or detracts from its theme. The decision to use a pop-up in a book project should not be an arbitrary one. An idea should demand dimension. A pop-up can provide just the right element of surprise, focus, and clarity to your idea. It can introduce a sense of play to a work, or serve as a counterpoint to a serious subject.

Sometimes I regret that I have no childhood memories of a favorite pop-up text. But in many ways I'm probably fortunate that I didn't discover the pop-up form until I had already embarked on a career as an artist; I recognized the potential of engineered paper along with the surprise. The mystery has been solved. I can easily look at most pop-ups and recognize the tricks that make them move. The pop-up form pushes beyond the flatness of the page to break into the realm of sculpture. Yet it all folds down into a neat little package known as a book. Fortunately, the magic remains.

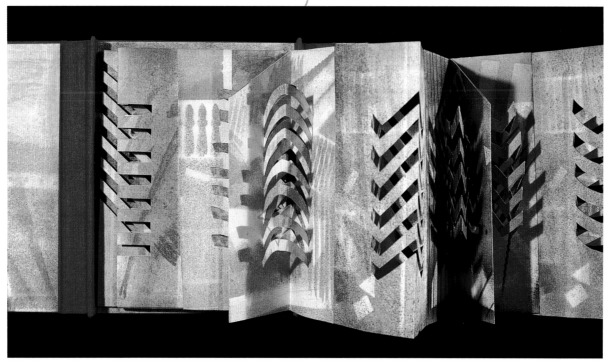

Rhythmic Notes on Seven Folds, 1990. 9 x 7½ x 58 inches (22.5 x 18.8 x 145 cm), extended. Paper plates; hand-cut pop-ups; offset lithography; one-of-a-kind.
Photos by the artist.

CAROL BARTON

Hands On

Carol demonstrates the engineering behind two pop-up structures. The V-fold pop-up works when the page is to be fully opened flat. The asymmetrical pop-up works when the page is opened half-way to 90°.

V-Fold Pop-Up

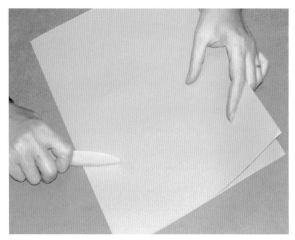

1. Folding the page or card base in half using a bone folder—the pop-up will be glued on this page.

2. Scissors cut the background cloud image for the pop-up. I add a 1-inch (2.5 cm) strip that will become the glue tab along the base of the image.

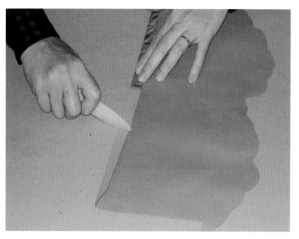

3. The 1-inch (2.5 cm) glue tab is folded back along the base of the cloud image. After folding the tab back it's pulled forward again.

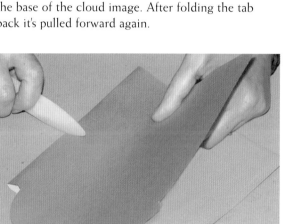

4. The cloud image is folded in half. This fold is positioned perpendicular to the glue tab.

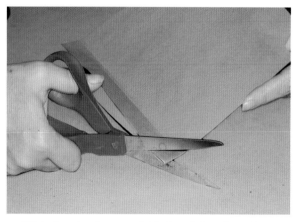

5. With the cloud image folded and the glue tab extended, I divide the glue tab in half at the centerfold by cutting a triangular notch in the tab. You have to be careful not to cut into the image.

6. The pop-up with the lower glue tab divided.

7. I visually position the folded pop-up on the opened page. It needs to lie at an angle to the page's centerfold with the center point of the glue-tab notch touching the centerfold. After positioning, the glue tabs are extended.

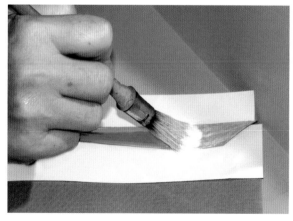

8. To protect the page, I place waste sheets under the top glue tab before brushing PVA on one side of the tab's surface. I use a glue stick for gluing models, but use only PVA for finished pieces.

9. Here I'm folding one side of the page down onto the glued tab. Afterward, I flip the folded page, open the other side, and repeat the same gluing sequence in steps 8 and 9 for the other glue tab.

10. With the gluing complete, the page opens to reveal the cloud image popping straight up off the page.

11. The completed pop-up with three layers of images titled *Weather: 50% Chance of Rain*.

Asymmetrical Pop-Up

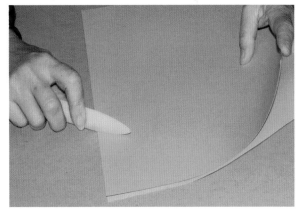

1. The page or card base where the pop-up will be glued is folded in half.

2. Using scissors to cut the background desert landscape for the pop-up. I add a 1-inch (2.5 cm) strip for a glue tab along the base of the image.

3. The 1-inch (2.5cm) glue tab is folded along the base of the desert landscape image.

4. To protect the page, I place waste sheets under the glue tab before brushing PVA onto the tab's surface.

5. With the base page open, the desert landscape is glued onto the left side of the page parallel to the centerfold of the card.

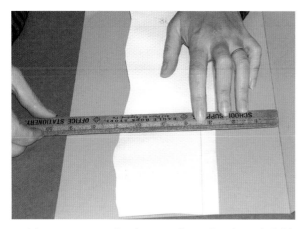

6. After measuring the distance from the glue tab fold in the desert landscape to the centerfold of the page, I add 1 inch (2.5 cm) to this distance. This is enough to allow me to make two ½-inch (1.3 cm) glue tabs.

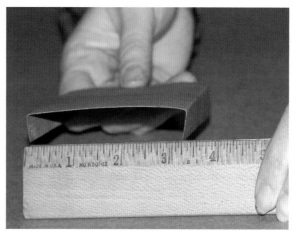

7. I cut a separate strip that is approximately 1 to 3 inches (2.5 to 7.5 cm) wide and to the length determined in step 6. Then I fold a ½-inch (1.3 cm) glue tab at either end of the strip's length.

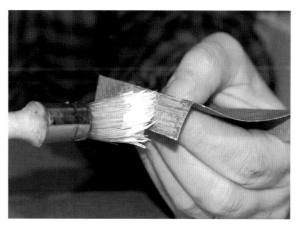

8. Applying PVA to one of the glue tabs on the separate strip.

9. When gluing the separate strip to the back side of the desert landscape, I place it parallel to the landscape base.

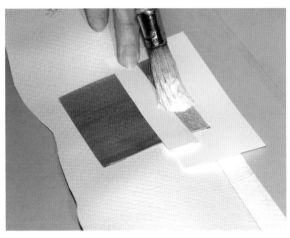

10. Before applying PVA to the separate strip's other glue tab, I place waste sheets under the strip.

11. Now the page is folded down on the glued tab.

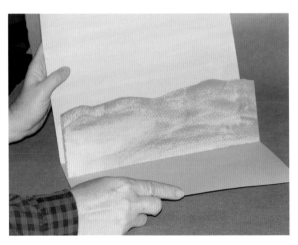

12. Here's the desert landscape when it pops up.

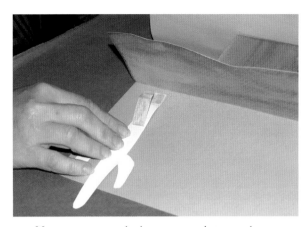

13. Using separate tabs between each image layer allows me to add other images in the same manner in front of the landscape.

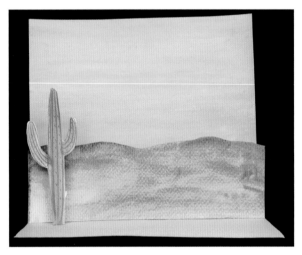

14. Adding a cactus is a natural complement to the desert scene.

15. The completed pop-up, titled *Weather: Hellishly Hot, No Sign of Relief,* has five image layers.

About the Artist

CAROL BARTON is a studio artist, curator, and teacher living and working in Bethesda, MD. She is on the faculty at the University of the Arts in Philadelphia, and has taught at art centers and institutions across the United States, including Rhode Island School of Design, Minnesota Center for Book Arts, the Smithsonian Institution, and Penland School of Crafts.

Carol publishes her own artist editions and has organized both local and national shows of artist's books. Her work is exhibited internationally and is in numerous collections, including the Library of Congress, the Museum of Modern Art, and the Victoria and Albert Museum in London. She served as curator for the Smithsonian Institution's exhibition "Science and the Artist's Book."

In 1999 Carol's artist's book edition *Vision Shifts* was published by the Borowsky Center in Philadelphia. She was awarded the Bogliasco Fellowship for a residency in Italy in the fall of 2000, during which time she worked on *Five Luminous Towers*. She was also awarded a residency by the Sacatar Foundation in Brazil for the fall of 2001. She is currently working on an artist's how-to book on paper engineering, which will be published in 2004.

Gallery

Imagine a library full of books with pages that refuse to lie flat. Instead, as you browse through each volume, the pages transform into a sculptural array of buildings, butterflies, plant forms, desserts. The photos in my gallery can only convey some of the excitement experienced when reading these dimensional "texts." But even this static display captures a bit of the wonder to be found between the covers of these artist-produced volumes.

Emily Martin's humorous pop-up editions often provide comment on her midwestern American lifestyle, while the sophisticated geometries in Sjoerd Hofstra's work illustrate his personal interests in architecture and structural design. Bonnie Stablecker uses pop-up forms as visual devices to focus her viewers' attention on specific topics or themes in her books, as here in her piece Warped Words. Wedding Cake, *by Dorothy Yule, is an amazing sculptural reenactment of a nuptial celebration, and her* Souvenirs of Great Cities *offers a miniature tour of four cities she and her sister Susan have lived in, citing their favorite attractions in each. Lois Morrison's* Endangered Species *provides political commentary on the environmental, health, and social dangers faced by children around the world. Children of each continent are shown floating on the petals of imaginary floral forms.*

All of these artists have deftly managed to push the pop-up beyond its origins as an entertainment novelty. These dimensional paper forms are integral elements in communicating both serious and satirical narrative themes, while retaining a sense of the fun that the pop-up form naturally evokes.

Emily Martin, *How Can I Live in Iowa?*, 1999. 5 x 6¾ inches (12.7 x 17.1 cm). Mohawk Superfine and Nideggen papers; mylar; watercolor; color pencils; drawings scanned and archival inkjet printed; four-layer carousel construction; house torn and reattached.
Photos by Meryl Marek.

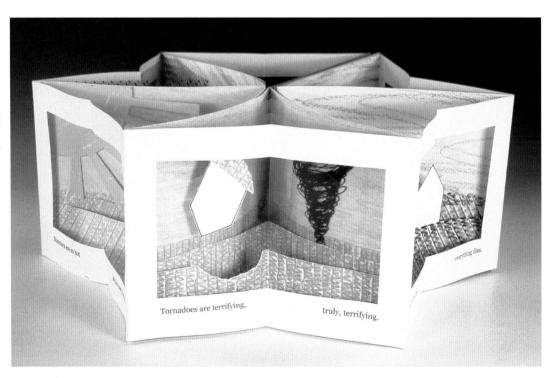

Dorothy Yule, *Wedding Cake Book,* 1995. Box: 5½ x 5½ inches (14 x 14 cm); assembled book: 9 inches (22.9 cm) tall. Boxed set of three concertinas with pop-up in each opening; images rubber-stamped with a gold embossing powder; text in gold ink.
Photos by the artist.

Bonnie Stahlecker,
Warped Words, 2002.
3⅜ x 4 inches
(8.6 x 10.2 cm).
Letterpress and
intaglio printed along
with intaglio images on
Somerset Book Cover;
both layers paste
painted; book cloth
covers with painted
board on top; double
accordion fold with
pop-ups and cut outs.
Photo by the artist.

Lois Morrison, *Endangered Species,*
1999. 7 x 8¾ x 11¼ inches
(17.8 x 22.2 x 28.6 cm). Assorted
archival papers; cloth over board cover;
color-copied pencil and crayon drawings, dry-matted and glued; hand cut
and assembled pop-ups shimmed with
strips of credit cards. *Photos by James Dee.*

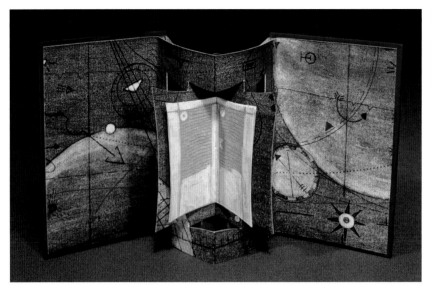

Bonnie Stahlecker, *Journey One,* 1995.
3 x 5 inches (7.6 x 12.7 cm). Intaglio
printed in ink with hand coloring added;
paste painted on back; painted board
covers; two-layer accordion fold with
pop-up in center fold. *Photo by the artist.*

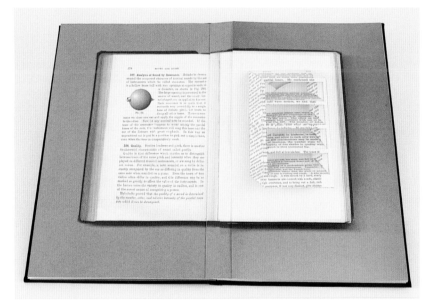

Sjoerd Hofstra, *6 Empty Bookcases,* 1996.
12¾ x 16½ inches (32.4 x 41.9 cm). Scanned images;
inkjet printed on Bristol two-ply smooth paper; various
pop-up techniques. *Photos by Tim Keating.*

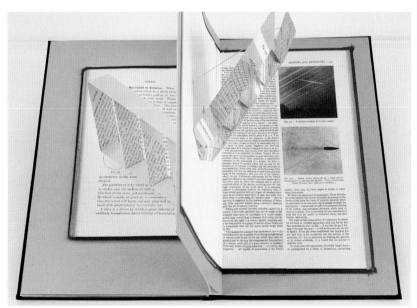

Emily Martin, *I Live in Iowa,*
1999.7 x 8½ x 3 inches (17.8 x
21.6 x 7.6 cm). Paste papers, rag
and flax papers, wire, cotton
thread; inkjet printed; various
pop-up techniques.
Photos by Meryl Marek.

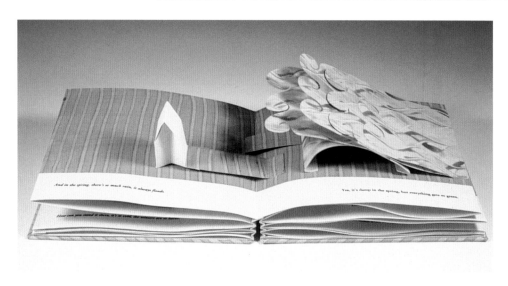

Carol Barton

Dorothy Yule, *Memories of Science,* 1996-present. 3 x 2¾ x 1¼ inches (7.6 x 6.9 x 3.2 cm). Laser printed on Mohawk Superfine and Superfine Cover; hand colored concertina structure with removable spine; French-folded folios of text and pop-up collages in alternate openings. *Photo by the artist.*

Dorothy Yule, *Souvenirs of Great Cities,* 1992-1996. Box: 5½ x 5½ inches (14 x 14 cm); books: 2½ x 2½ inches (6.4 x 6.4 cm). Letterpress printed in five colors on Mohawk Superfine Cover with photopolymer plates made from computer separations; concertina structures with removable spines, text and pop-ups on both sides. Illustrations by Susan Hunt Yule. *Photos by the artist.*

Susan E. King

By remaining open to the content that surrounds her—in dreams, random thoughts, and overheard conversation— Susan E. King creates books that are rich in meaning. In describing her process, she presents the relationships between content and intent and their impact on making technical and structural decisions for the book.

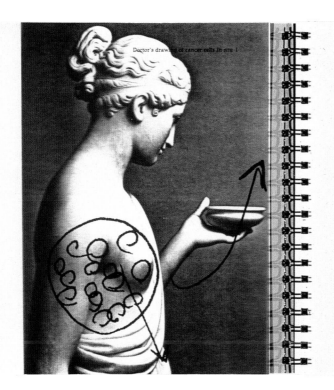

Doctor's drawing of cancer cells *In situ* i

Start Here

TREADING THE **MaZe**

AN ARTIST'S BOOK OF DAZE

SUSAN E. KING

MONTAGE 93: INTERNATIONAL FESTIVAL OF THE IMAGE,
ROCHESTER, NEW YORK
1993

Today the need to
travel — especially to
places
unfamiliar and
even unpleasant —
motivates much of the
art discussed here and
can be seen as part of
a general social anxi-
ety. Some artists are
inspired by what they
see and return home
to develop it; others
work while they
travel; others make
travel their work.
The impulse toward
constant movement is

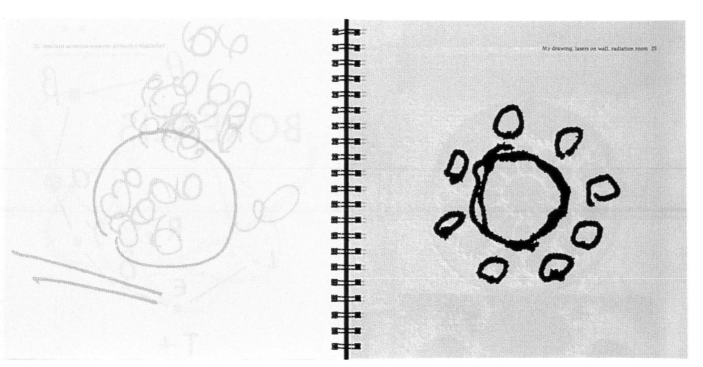

My drawing, lasers on wall, radiation room 25

Treading the Maze, 1993. 7⁵⁄₁₆ x 8½ inches (17.6 x 25.6 cm). Detail: Title page, Goddess Hebe. Offset printed with two photocopy transparanecies; double-wire spiral binding. *Photo by John Kiffee.*

Finding, Following, and Allowing the Process

Redressing the Sixties, (art) lessons à la mode, 1986. 9⅛ by 10¾ inches (22.8 x 26.9 cm). Detail: Maid Marion Dress. Paste-paper; leterpress; Coptic binding.
Photo by John Kiffee.

An art center I know reports that many of their book arts' students master the techniques of bookbinding but feel lost when it comes to generating content for getting started in their own studios. The best advice I can give is that the most productive route to take is to inch ahead on the dark road of making art, and to find your way as you go.

For example, I get frustrated with grant applications that ask me to tell every detail about the book I'm proposing. What I want is support to find that answer myself. I'd rather abandon myself to process and tolerate a certain amount of not knowing exactly where I am along the road. Not everyone is willing or able to take on this challenge. But given a try, this approach may enliven your work.

My exploration of content and intent began when my college art teacher gave an assignment to create a collage that expressed an emotion or state of mind. We worked directly with the simplest materials: a piece of tagboard and pieces of junk from scrap boxes. The results were compelling. It was one of the most meaningful projects during my time at the university.

In the early '60s I joined the Feminist Studio Workshop where I was encouraged to make art with content. It was a time when women artists in particular had a lot to say—the women I knew certainly did. Making books allowed me to write, make images, print, design, and bookbind; yet the projects that held my interest and captured my imagination delved into content along with technical proficiency.

Technical training became a handmaiden to content, and I discovered content was all around me—in dreams, random thoughts, and overheard conversation. My job was to stay open to the process. If I needed to learn some technical aspect, I would learn it. For example, I took a two-day workshop, printed a business card, and from there taught myself to print a book.

As writing became more a part of my work, I joined a writer's group, and my writing got stronger. I saw how one image led to another and that the subject of my writing was just an opener to get me to some other place. It became clear I couldn't accurately predict the result. Working this way was extremely liberating. I began to realize that what I needed to do was to pay attention—to pay homage—to the images and bits of writing that came my way and called my name. As my husband likes to say, "it's simple, not easy."

If anxiety set in, it helped to think of my process as an experiment. (It's a great thing to tell nosey family and friends who demand to know *WHAT* you are doing.) The corner of Hollywood and Vine capture your attention? What would happen if you hung out there every Saturday morning for four months, or if you surrounded yourself with images and writing about that part of Hollywood? You don't have to know the answer. Your job is to find out. Love a postcard someone sent you from the Uffizzi? The one hanging on your studio wall? Nurture that attraction, invest some time in it, and see where it takes you.

The joy of working this way is not knowing what the result will be or where the art making process will ultimately take you. So while I can't predict your result, I can show you the steps, missteps, and the flavor of working this way by using one of my recent letterpress printed books titled *Redressing the Sixties, (art) lessons à la mode* (see photo on page 92), as an example. The following is a good study of how content affects technical and structural decisions, and how those decisions shape the intent of the book.

People who shop in antiques stores know the thrill of discovery, and that's exactly how I felt when I saw a brown, side stabbed book on a bookseller's table. Larger than my hand and smaller than a bottle of sake, it contained page after page of old kimono fabric samples pasted to Japanese paper sheets. Japanese

New York City (My Mother Told Me), 1994. 11½ x 48 inches (28.8 x 120 cm). Japanese paper, gouache, laser prints; letterpress printed; Japanese double-hinged screen binding.

Salem Witch Trial
Memorial, 1994. 8 x
57½ inches (20 x 143.8
cm). Lasar prints,
gouache, painted
Mingei-shi paper;
Japanese double-
hinge screen binding.

old Hollywood. And although I didn't purchase the little book, it stayed with me as well. I was intrigued with the idea of having fabric attached to the pages of a book. The fabric added a richness and tactile quality to each page that couldn't be matched by mere ink and paper alone. Later I would analyze my reaction to the small fabric samples: the clothing made from them was ephemeral and yet held history—of the body, of the style of the time, of the life and situation of the wearer. But that was much later. All I knew then was that I had a yen for the little book. And, although still somewhat vague and indefinable, I knew the feeling was somehow tied to my love of fabric.

characters, letterpress printed on each page, appeared to relate sample information. I don't read Japanese but I immediately fell in love with this book.

I saw the book when I was attending an antiquarian book fair held at the Ambassador Hotel in Los Angeles. With its lavish mirrored rooms in the Regency style, the Ambassador embodied the glamour of old Hollywood. One could easily imagine the stars of the '30s and '40s there: Ingrid Bergman wearing women's wide-leg trousers, strolling through the airy passageways in that carefree way she had on screen; Gregory Peck peering into a gilt mirror to adjust his tie.

It was thrilling to browse the booksellers' tables lined with literary first editions and esoteric tomes. At the time, I had just set up my own letterpress shop. My interest in printing had taken me into the worlds of the English fine press tradition and classic book design. Yet I was living in Los Angeles, which looks not to England, but across the Pacific to Japan. So things Japanese were on my mind as well. The influence of Japanese culture is certainly felt in Los Angeles, from the yukatas (cotton kimonos) and Bento lunch boxes one can buy in Little Tokyo, to the Japanese patterned papers available in art stores. Clothing, lunch, and art.

The pleasure of that Saturday stayed with me, wrapped in the memory of the luxurious old hotel and

I've always responded to the beauty of fabric, as if every bolt or piece of yard goods was a small work of art. As a teenager, I started collecting fabric to make dresses. My aunt introduced me to thrift stores where I bought stylish dresses and suits from the '40s for pennies. Years later, a suitcase full of those handmade and vintage dresses followed me to California. Too outdated to wear, I couldn't bring myself to throw them away since they were a time capsule of my life as a young art student. Slowly I developed the idea of transforming my dresses into a book. Each dress, after all, had a story—from fabric shopping trips with my mother to sewing dresses for college while watching old movies on TV. (Ingrid Bergman, I couldn't help noticing between stitching side darts, looked glamorous on a refugee's budget in Casablanca.) Each piece of clothing was also set in the drama of its decade, attached to events ranging from the launch of Sputnik, to the assassination of John F. Kennedy, to the Watergate trials.

At this point I knew I wanted to make the book in multiples. What I didn't know was exactly how I wanted the book to feel. What method of printing would I use? I could imagine using a swatch of each garment in a letterpress book. This would give me several layers of tactile quality: the type impressed on the paper, the paper itself (could I use handmade paper?), the fabric pinned or glued to the page. If I went with other reproduction choices, such as offset or laser printing, the book would be cooler. I could scan or use a copy camera to photograph the fabric, which would give me the option of using a whole sleeve of a dress in each book, but I'd lose the tactile quality I admired in the original Japanese book.

I thought of Joan Lyons' work *Prom* made during a hectic week when she had to choose between making a piece for an exhibit or a dress for her daughter. She placed the pattern pieces for the dress on the copy camera as she sewed the dress, making life-sized color separations of the dress in pieces. She ended up with a suite of large offset prints of the dress pieces for her book, and a finished prom dress for her daughter. I liked the large areas of fabric in Joan's work—but I kept seeing my own project as a letterpress book. My main concern was that the cost of the book printed on handmade paper, with lots of handwork involved, would be quite high.

When I actually started the book, I began with the writing because I was sure it would take the longest. This meant sitting in front of the computer for an hour each morning and just starting. I knew I would write and rewrite. I'm convinced that the effort put into rewriting is the secret to making the material better. The writing took on a life of its own. It stalled for a long while. When I picked it up again, Ingrid Bergman and Kim Novak took early leading roles in the manuscript as I wrote about watching late night movies that shaped my child's view of women, fashion, and the world. I transcribed dialogue as I watched all the Ingrid Bergman movies I could find. I read about women's movies of the '30s and '40s, and read books on clothing's link to culture. I started to visualize how the text would look on the page of the finished book.

I eventually received a grant from the National Museum of Women in the Arts Library Fellows to produce the project as a letterpress book. With the printing decision made, I could think about the book's form. I knew the side stab binding of the Japanese book was untenable; our Western paper is too stiff for

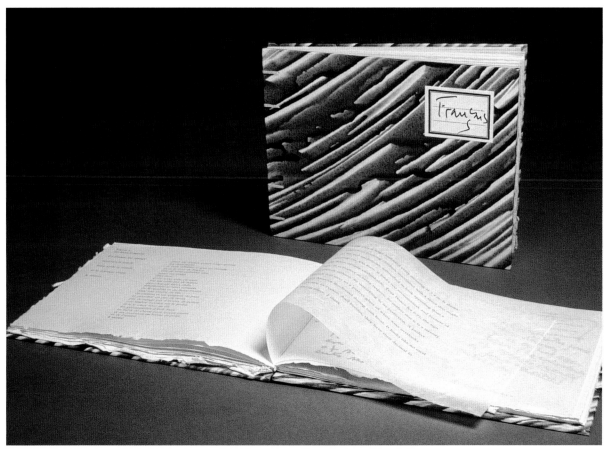

Say, See, Bone, Lessons from French, with Jean Gabriel Adloff, 1989. 5½ x 7½ inches (13.8 x 8.8 cm). Letterpress printed on handmade paper; Coptic binding; boards covered in paste paper; Japanese paper overlays. *Photo by John Kiffee.*

these bindings and if you use stiff paper your book will snap shut. My third book, *Pacific Legend*, suffers from this common mistake. Besides, I wanted a structure that would allow the book to open flat, and permit a double-page spread to be seen as a chapter, thus using the structure to reinforce the content. Turn the page and you turn to a new chapter. Turn the page and the world of the reader changes.

There was another reason for choosing a flat structure, such as a Coptic binding. I'd used Coptic binding with *Say, See, Bone, Lessonsfrom French* because it reminded me of a thick clunky French notebook, the kind with blue marbled paper on the cover. I could see this new book as part of a trilogy, starting with *Lessons from the South*. Perhaps that type of title would work for this book as yet unnamed (*Lessons from Fashion? What Artists Wore?*).

I always make a dummy for any new book. It allows me to see and feel the way a book might work. I can spot design flaws and make minor adjustments at the beginning stages that would be difficult to make later on. For this book, I made a dummy with materials on hand. I knew the board thickness was wrong, but I'd change that later. In piecing together paper to cover the board, I ended up using some gaudy paste

paper for the cover's interior and a marbled paper in the Spanish pattern for the cover. I thought its slightly seasick pattern might just work to evoke the psychedelic feel of the period I was writing about. I ordered sample paper from the mill to determine the size of the text block. The color I wanted, lavender, wasn't in stock, and they sent paper that was the right weight, but was foamy green. It was a favorable accident since I ended up liking the green better (Was this like trying on dresses? I'd just stumbled across some new spring color I thought my book would never wear, and I liked it!).

When I make a dummy I start by folding the parent sheet, the whole sheet of paper, into sections. Using good paper (i.e. the paper I'll use in the final book, even if it's a second to begin with), I can feel how the paper folds and whether it lays flat when folded at various sizes. It's a false economy to save a few dollars to use cheaper paper at this point—there is too much information to be learned from the good paper. I started folding the paper to see what size of rectangles I could get from this particular paper. I try to get the largest book I can out of the parent sheet. For me, using the whole sheet is an elegant solution. In commercial printing, standard sized books are made this way. The number of folds made in the sheet determines the page size. None of the paper is wasted. But artists aren't bound by these standard sizes. Sometimes it's really important to have a square book, or an extremely tall and skinny book. You'll probably end up with lots of waste this way. Sometimes, by working with folding the sheet early on, you can get close to that square book you wanted by changing the dimensions slightly.

The deckle was uneven and quite exaggerated in places. I hated to lose it (Printer's joke: Printer takes a book to the binder and tells him to save the deckle. Printer comes back and the binder hands her the book with the deckle cut off and carefully saved.). As I folded the paper, I realized I could use the deckles to hide and reveal text. By folding the deckles in toward the spine at the fore edge of the book, I would have an extra surface on which to print or to attach something—always a bonus in my books. I'm constantly looking for ways the structure can support the text. I could use this area for quotes and small pieces of writing I'd been collecting that weren't part of the main text, but could float nearby. Also, having fabric samples glued to the pages would add bulk, and folding the paper at the fore edge might help offset the bulkiness. I knew this kind of maneuver would affect the finished binding, but I'd know more when I got the dummy finished.

I printed this book on a letterpress, but there was too much text to handset in metal type. I used QuarkXpress, a computer graphics program, to lay out the book. From designing poetry books, I knew it was useful to work with the extremes of a text, and so I laid out the shortest and longest sections of prose. Once I chose a typeface, I began to mock up the entire book with title page, all pages of text, and end matter. I saw how many pages were in the book, and estimated exactly how much paper I needed, then ordered substantially more to leave room for some major problem or mistake that would require reprinting. It's always easier and cheaper to order extra paper up front. Lack of paper can substantially reduce your edition when you're short of copies of just one section.

Since the foam-green paper brought a different feeling to the book, I saw I needed something more sophisticated than the gaudy marbled and paste papers I used for the cover dummy. I was looking forward to making marbled paper, but started to feel like I needed to go with paste paper alone. I had a sample where I'd drawn on top of a paste paper that provided a good point of departure for creating the new sheet. I experimented with both color choice and application on a new batch of papers. Golden fluid acrylics are especially good for making colored paste. The color I wanted wasn't available in the fluid viscosity, but I used the Golden jar paints and mixed them with methylcellulose paste. I kept track of the colors since I knew I would need to make several gallons of colored paste for the final edition of 150 books. I drew on the new sheet with a standard drawing pencil and realized that I could wrap the drawing around the book. The

Redressing the Sixties, (art) lessons à la mode, 1986. Detail: ceramic drawing.

new paper reminded me of the Sol Lewitt drawings I saw as an art student—it felt more sophisticated and added a reference to the art world of the '60s and '70s.

Since so much of the book was about sewing, I gathered sewing notions to play with. I cut up the clothing into sample-sized swatches, being careful to include pattern design on some pieces (Was I really going to be able to cut up some of those wonderful garments?). Most pieces would be pasted down. Glass-head pins, I soon discovered, could be used as page turners, and as a way to attach a piece of lace that couldn't be glued down. A strip of the pink leather glove I bought at the street market in Florence in 1969 was attached by lacing it through the handmade paper flap, allowing the reader to handle it.

I toyed with the idea of recreating a label from a vintage suit jacket, and this led me to make a small badge out of Japanese paper for one page of the book. On another flap in the book I used Japanese paper to represent abstract painting. I collaged a strip of paper on top and wrapped it around the flap to encourage the reader to turn the flap and look on the other side. I wanted to make something that embodied Japanese culture, perhaps the feel of stoneware pottery that represented my experience of studying ceramics? I decided to draw a tea bowl— an image of something I studied—on sandpaper with a Japanese brush dipped

in gouache, as if I were painting a scroll. This was easy to attach to a sheet, and added more drawing to the book.

I made a test print on the sample paper to see if I could print the book dry without dampening the paper, but the test looked uneven and I knew I had to dampen the paper. This was not good news, since the extra step of dampening meant a stricter printing schedule—but it produced a much better page. Some fabrics were too delicate to be glued. A vintage crepe blouse was already in shreds, but I still wanted to include it. I cut delicate ovals with a punch and laced them to a page with silk buttonhole twist, something I'd picked up at the notions counter. After the pages were collated, and the covers boxed up, I sent them to the binders in San Diego who did the Coptic binding.

Looking over the printed book, I'm surprised to see how I've created an intimate artist's sketchbook using fabric and stories about sewing and watching old movies. It is a book that holds an exuberant time in history the way our favorite clothing holds memory for each of us and the culture at large. The content, intent, and technical considerations came together, some by fortunate accident, others by adjusting to the changing needs of the work, but all by remaining open to the process.

Hands On

Susan shows how content can influence technical and structural decisions by demonstrating the steps to creating her book *Redressing the Sixties, (art) lessons à la mode.*

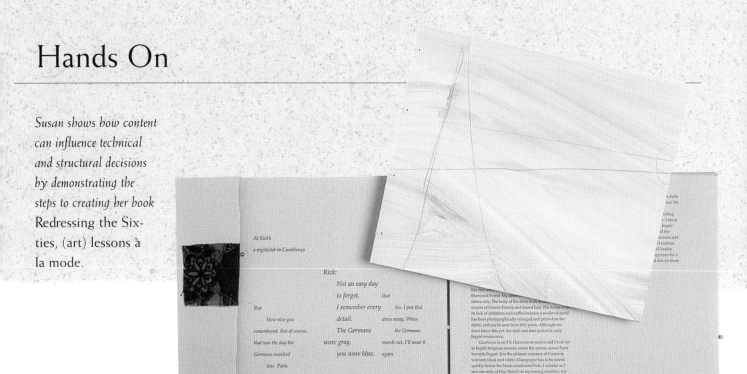

Content and Intent

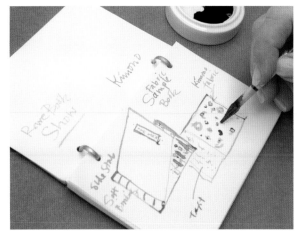

1. A sketch of the Japanese kimono sample book that inspired me reminds me of the elements I want in the new book.

2. Gathering materials gives me a sense of the qualities I want in the book, including the tactile quality of real fabric, linen, handmade paper, and silk thread.

3. To determine what binding to use, I compare the binding of a Japanese side stab book (below) to Coptic binding (above). This shows that Coptic binding will let the pages lie flat, a structural element I want for enhancing the content.

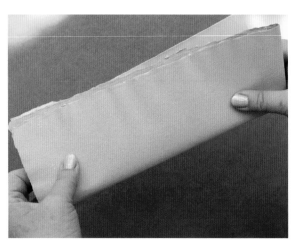

4. While making a paper dummy is essential for the defining the structure, it also allows other thoughts about aspects of the book to emerge.

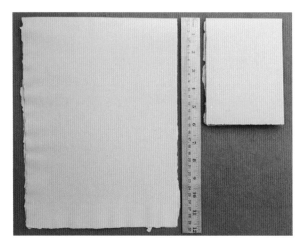

5. After measuring the dummy, I determine that the shape is right for the book but the size is wrong and will need to be adjusted.

6. The dummy shows that the book board is too thin. Since scrap materials were used for the dummy, a thicker board can be used for the actual book.

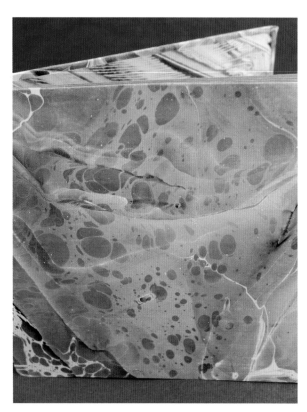

7. Using scrap papers for the dummy cover combine traditional marble papers and paste papers. At this stage, I think it can work since the paper will make a gaudy cover that resembles the acid rock posters of the '60s.

8. The paper mill sends a foamy-green paper (bottom) because it doesn't have the original color (middle) I wanted. I find that I actually prefer the green over my first choice and it changes the way I think about the colored paste paper that will be used for the cover (top).

9. The whole sheet, known as the parent sheet, is folded for the dummy. Folding shows what size rectangles can come from this particular paper.

10. The edges are folded to use as a flap. I decide to incorporate some of the deckles into the structure of the book to hide and reveal text at the fore-edge.

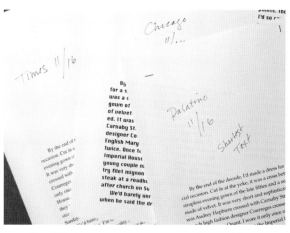

11. QuarkXpress generates the type. It quickly produces model pages in different type styles and sizes that allow me to make decisions about what to use. Afterward, the files generated are made into film and the film made into polymer plates for printing on a Vandercook SP20 letterpress.

12. Because the paper is thick, and to avoid any binding problems, each signature is made as one section of four pages.

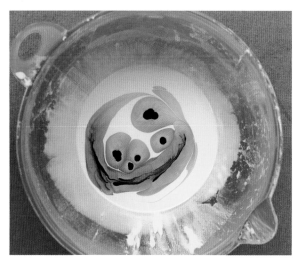

13. A paper made in an earlier workshop is the inspiration for making a new paste paper that won't clash with the foam-green. I use Golden acrylics to make a color test.

14. Once the paste paper is made and dried it needs to be flattened. I place it in a book press I've made from sheets of ¾-inch (1.9 cm) birch plywood.

15. Drawing on the paste paper makes it resemble the paper that inspired it.

16. The paper is wrapped around the book to make sure the drawn line flows as a continuous stroke.

17. These are some of the sewing notions gathered for the book.

18. One spontaneous idea was to use glass-head pins as page turners. Here they're tested in their new capacity.

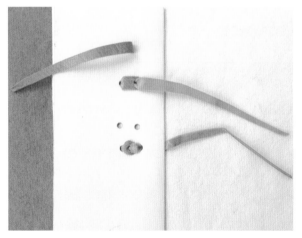

19. A small book of closures made in a Hedi Kyle workshop acts as a reference for finding a way to attach a piece of leather glove.

SUSAN E. KING

20. The small piece of glove is attached to a paper flap.

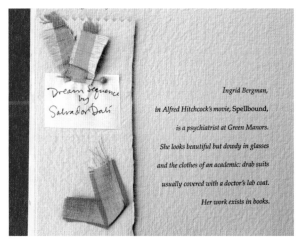

21. A label from old clothes becomes the genesis for a badge that will appear on one page.

22. To represent an abstract painting of the era, Japanese paper stands in for painted surfaces.

23. An extra strip of paper is used as a collage on top of the Japanese paper to give the reader a clue to turn the flap.

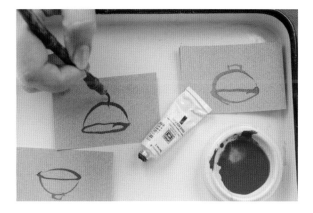

24. For a section on studying Japanese ceramics, I paint an image of a tea bowl on sandpaper. The sandpaper acts as a fabric substitute providing a surface on which to paint.

25. Using a polymer plate, I make a dry-print sample on the press to see if the book can be printed without dampening the paper.

I sit sewing at a card table in the TV room on a Tuesday morning. The dress is simple but has one historic detail, a balloon of cloth falling fro raglan sleeves, modeled after costumes in pain of the Northern Renaissance. (France and the Netherlands as compared to the Italian.) I know from my art history studies. I've been scanning of paintings for months, using stylistic differen such as the surface of a painting here, the background there, to identify a lifetime of work. Sometimes it is possible to use a hairstyle, the position of a lap dog or the swag of rotting frui

shopping where I worked every night in my blue smock I'd found just the right color 32" zipper, and the thing was made.

I had on this dress, just finished, with its paisley swirls of hot pink, yellow and acid green. I took shortcu through the art building, making sure I passed through the studio area. So constant was my path I remember no other routes, no other doors. I was on my way from the Art library to the Student Center, a modern ugly box tacked on the back of a more graceful, earlier building.

I passed through the studio section of the Art building, and there was my advisor. All forty plus years of hi slouched against the doorjamb of his studio. He watched me walk the length of the hall, down the ramp by our

26. The resulting dry print looks uneven. I decide to go back to dampening, which will mean a much stricter printing schedule.

27. Every other sheet is dampened with a sponge and distilled water, then the dampened sheets are stacked on a piece of clear acrylic.

28. The sheets will rest overnight in a damp box, in this case a plywood box with wet sponges along the walls. Tip: An under-the-bed plastic storage box makes an excellent damp box.

29. The results of the damp printing look much better than the dry.

30. After the finished paste paper is cut to size, I glue the boards. Numbering the boards as I cover the exteriors ensures that the pencil drawing on the paste paper will continue around the spine to the adjacent board.

31. Once each section is printed and folded, the fabric is attached to the pages. PVA works best to hold heavy fabric to handmade paper.

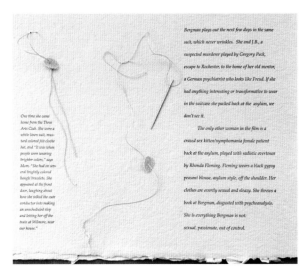

32. I used silk buttonhole twist to lace delicate ovals of vintage crepe onto a book flap.

Some of the tools used in making the book.

Redressing the Sixties, (art) lessons à la mode, 1986. Detail: Maid Marion dress.

About the Artist

SUSAN E. KING is an artist and writer who started making books after she moved to Southern California in the 1970s to be part of the experimental Feminist Studio Workshop. She grew up in the South, in a family of storytellers. Southern oral tradition and history, and writing about place often appear in her work. Trained as a sculptor and potter, she brings sculptural aspects to making printed and one-of-a-kind artists' books.

Her work is in major collections, including The Getty Center Research Institute Library, Bel Air, CA; the Bibliothèque Nationale, Paris, France; the Museum of Modern Art Library, New York City; and the Victoria and Albert Museum National Art Library, London. She lives in rural Kentucky with her husband and two cats.

Gallery

Philip Zimmermann,
Nature Abhors, 2003. 5½ x
5½ inches (13.8 x 13.8 cm).
HP Indigo digital printing
on Tintoretto paper; hand
bound. *Photos by the artist.*

*B*etsy Davids' inspiring and thoughtful work set a standard for me from the beginning. It's grounded in unusual combinations of literary, fine printing, and performance traditions, yet always feels contemporary. We share a love of travel and the imaginal world. Joan Lyons' feminist artist's books were some of the earliest I saw and admired in the 1970s. I wish we lived closer. Although I collect her books, I don't see her luscious prints often enough.

Terry Braunstein's work with collage and altered books always intrigue and move me. Her poignant placement of figures from the everyday world into the fantastic interiors of her books make me wonder about the mysteries of life.

Phil Zimmermann's angst ridden High Tension, presents a portrait of the artist's face as Everyman, in a narrative at once touching and amusing. Zimmermann is one of the few book artists I know whose use of the Macintosh computer makes artistic sense. Yet his work remains "true" to some of the early ideals of artist's bookworks, such as large printed multiple editions.

Scott McCarney's book, Memory Loss, is a masterpiece of content and form. He's deftly transformed the traumatic event of his brother's brain damage and made art that takes us to the beginning of language. It works on every level. Although we share many interests, I never know what Bonnie O'Connell will produce next. I've watched her move from traditional fine letterpress printing to artist's books, collage, and now sculptural bookworks. The Anti-Warhol Museum is a museum in the shape of a star. It proposes to raise money for the needy from the DE-accession of Warhol's work.

Katherine Ng's work has ties to her Chinese-American heritage and delights us with its form. But don't expect innocuous fortunes in those prettily boxed fortune cookies. Her work is often literally a Chinese puzzle, with content woven inside. Peter Madden's work always reminds me of early illuminated books, embellished here with pieces of ephemera from our modern life. His poetic bookworks remind us of the physicality of books before printing flattened the type to the page. Ruth Laxson's typographic work has ties to concrete poetry and Russian Constructivist typography. Her work simply bebops across the printed page, and is always a joy to behold.

Philip Zimmermann, *Nature Abhors,* 2003.

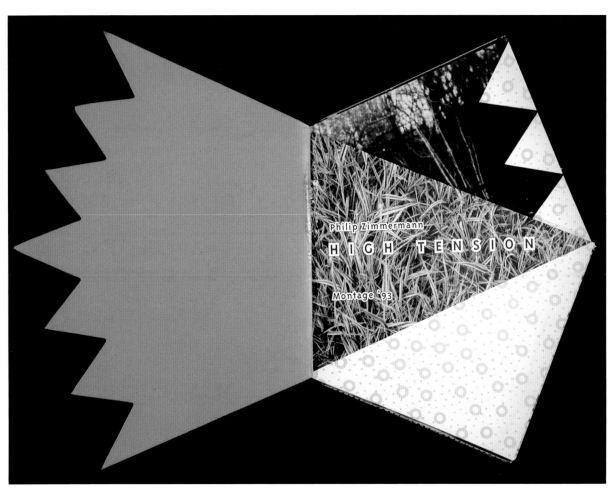

Philip Zimmermann, *High Tension,* 1993. 5½ x 8 inches (13.8 x 20 cm). Die-cut, three-color offset lithography on
Warren Patina paper; three-color tritone foil-stamped and die-cut cover; Smythe-sewn binding. *Photo by the artist.*

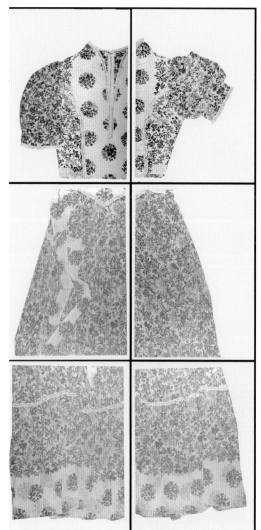

Joan Lyons, *Prom,* 1979. 17 x 22 inches (43.2 x 55.8 cm). Composite view. Screenless offset lithograph. *Photo by the artist.*

Katherine Ng, *Fortune Ate Me,* 1992. 5 x 7 x 1½ inches (12.7 x 17.8 x 3.8 cm). Letterpress printed on Strathmore bristol board; fortunes on Sequoia Text, using hand-set News Gothic and Bembo type; binding is modified pink pastry boxes tied with red string from Chinese deli. *Photos by the artist.*

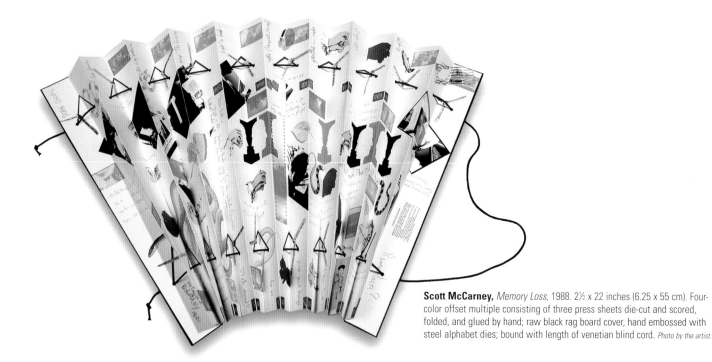

Scott McCarney, *Memory Loss,* 1988. 2½ x 22 inches (6.25 x 55 cm). Four-color offset multiple consisting of three press sheets die-cut and scored, folded, and glued by hand; raw black rag board cover, hand embossed with steel alphabet dies; bound with length of venetian blind cord. *Photo by the artist.*

Terry Braunstein, *Egg-Plant,*
2001. 9 x 6 x 2 inches (22.9 x
15.2 x 5 cm). Photomontage;
mixed media; sculpted altered
book. *Photo by the artist.*

Bonnie O'Connell, *The Anti-Warhol
Museum: Proposals for the Socially Responsible Disposal of Warholia,* 1993. 4⅝ x 6
inches (11.6 x 15 cm). Four-color offset diecut
accordion. *Photos by Denise Brady.*

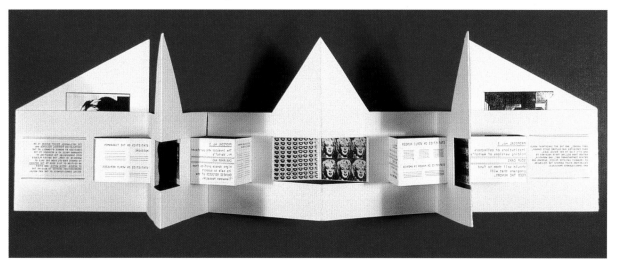

Bonnie O'Connell, *Raised Cord Binding: Another Visual Pun on the Descriptive Terminology of Bookbinding,* 2002. 14 x 13 x 3 inches (35 x 32.5 x 7.5 cm). Handmade flax and oak leaf paper, hemp cord, linen thread, bookcloth and board covers, African porcupine quills, copper tubing, mahogany. *Photo by Larry Gawel.*

Peter Madden, *Garden Shadows,* 1995. 10½ x 15 inches (26.3 x 37.5 cm). Covers: slate and copper; text: dyed cynotypes, solvent transfers; embossing and stitching on paper and cotton. *Photos by Tracy Storer.*

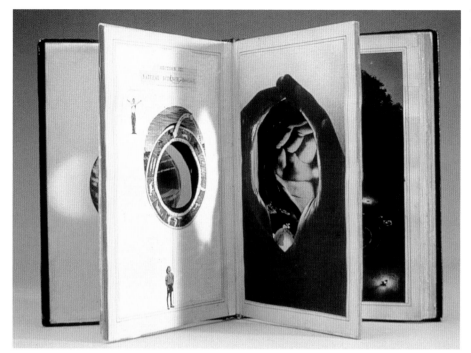

Terry Braunstein, *Circle of the Sciences,* 1988. 10 x 7 x 2 inches (25.4 x 17.8 x 5 cm). Photomontage, mixed media; sculpted altered book.
Photo by Victoria Damrel.

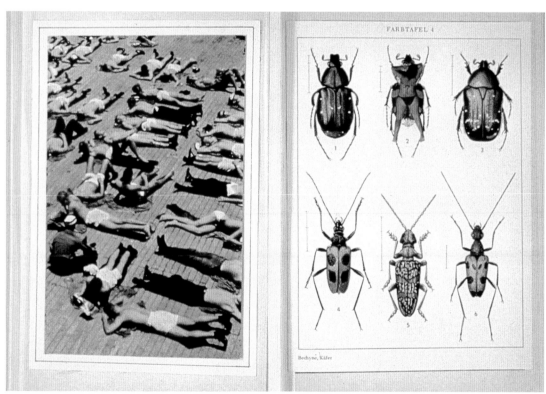

Terry Braunstein, *Metamorphoses,* 1993. 6 x 4 x 1 inches (15.2 x 10.2 x 2.5 cm).

Terry Braunstein, *Journeys Through Bookland,* 1991. 8 x 5 x 2 inches (20.3 x 12.7 x 5 cm). Mixed media, sculpture; photomontage; altered book. *Photo by Victoria Damrel.*

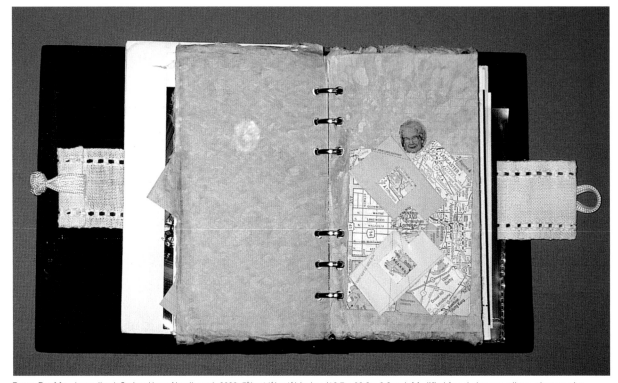

Betsy Davids, *Journalbook Series: Heart Needlework,* 2000. 7¾ x 14½ x 1½ inches (19.7 x 36.8 x 3.8 cm). Modified found planner, collage, photographs; embroidery. *Photo by the artist.*

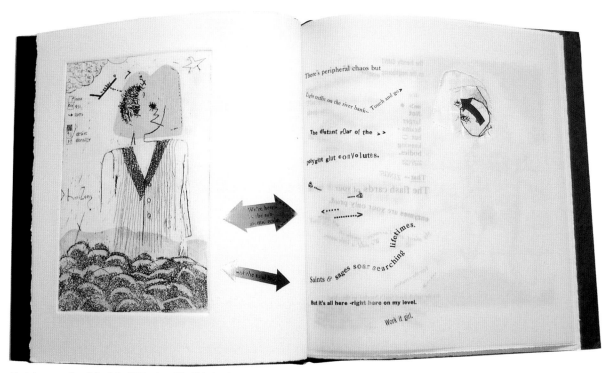

Ruth Laxson, *Retell the Tale*, 1997. 12 x 12¼ x ½ inches (30.5 x 31.1 x 1.3 cm). Rines BFK and UV Ultra II paper; etching; typography. *Photos by Terrylyn Marshall.*

Ruth Laxson, *A Hunderd Years of Lex Flex*, 2003. 10⅞ x 8¼ x ½ inches (27.6 x 21 x 1.3 cm). Mohawk vellum paper; offset printing. *Photos by Terrylyn Marshall.*

Hedi Kyle

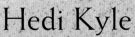

H
Hedi Kyle's books are lauded as
innovative and inspirational. Known
as the master of folded structure, she
flawlessly transforms a sheet of paper
into a book using only a bone folder
and her accomplished hands. As a
conservator, she is dedicated to
preserving the lives of books; as
an artist she lets us see their soul.

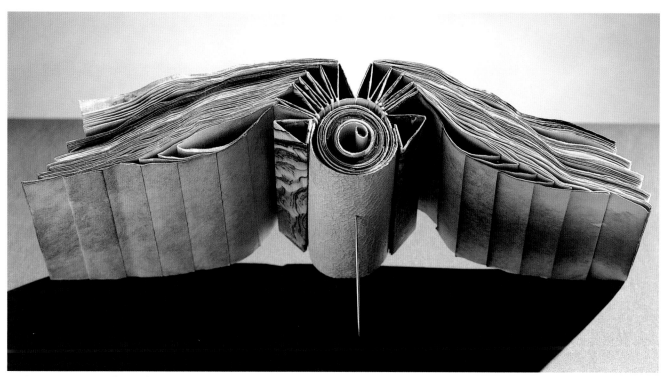

The Big Island, 1997-2004. 8½ x 6 x 2½ inches (21.6 x 15.2 x 6.4 cm). Various handmade and marbled papers, Firenze paper soaked in Iron Gall ink and brushed with bleach and dye; images are rubbed, printed, stenciled and collaged in an ongoing process. *Photo by Paul Warchol.*

Campus Specimen, 1999. 18 x 5 x ¾ inches (45.7 x 12.7 x 1.9 cm). Seedpod, telephone pages, yellow pad sheets painted with methylcellulose and graphite, bamboo leaves; burning, stenciling, collage, pages fastened around seedpod. *Photo by Paul Warchol.*

Behold the Fold

Train Log, 1996.
6½ x 6 x 2 inches
(16.5 x 15.2 x 5 cm).
Various crimped, dyed,
and painted papers,
leather, wooden stick;
colored pencil writing;
rolled-up computer
generated text, codex
and scroll construction.
Photo by Paul Warchol.

As a conservator, I look at books in a different way than I do as an artist. First of all, they are objects in need of care. I have seen books in deplorable condition, sometimes nothing more than decrepit relics. They have been damaged by fire and water, attacked by insects, exposed to dust and dirt, and subjected to unbearable temperatures. Left to self-destruct because of their inherent acidity, millions of books slowly burn to death, fall apart, crumble to dust.

With preservation options ranging from repair and rebinding to stabilizing and housing in archival enclosures, I am responsible for preserving all physical evidence. Taking the future use of the book into account, its value and its place in time, I have to decide when to interfere, if at all, with its structural integrity. I've come to believe that certain books should never be restored. Like ancient ruins they are infused with an awesome beauty reflecting a lost craft and distant culture.

In the process of examining books to make the right treatment decisions, I often stumble upon unexpected discoveries. These might be little-known binding techniques, strange materials, fantastic end sheets,

unusual typography, notations or marginalia—not to mention anything trapped between the pages. From insects to pressed plants, hair, feathers, or scraps of ephemera, something precious meant to remain hidden is now revealed. As you can see, the definition of the book as a medium of information goes beyond conventional interpretation.

When the decision is made to take certain books apart, I feel like a doctor carefully separating layers with the scalpel, softening and peeling linings from the spine. Since it was common practice among binders in older times to recycle manuscripts and printed materials for spine and board linings, I know another surprise awaits me. Sometimes during the repair process, fragments of text and images appear. As I release them from their time capsule, I invade a secret place and occasionally find a real treasure. I conceive the book as a repository, holding clues that reach far beyond the original intent.

Being in touch with old books on a day-to-day basis enables me to reconstruct binding techniques from different historical periods and cultures. I have the key to accessing a manifold repertoire of book formats. While it is challenging to devise conservation bindings based on traditional prototypes, devising bindings for freely associated structures imposes its own limitations.

In the early 1970s, institutions such as Franklin Furnace and Printed Matter in New York City, became important outlets for the artist's books genre. Such places presented a prolific output of wide-ranging subject matter to address the curious and open-minded reader. There, where I was able to browse and handle the books undisturbed, I experienced a new way of reading. I found that books with exotic inclusions or those made from unusual materials, which lent the books a tactile quality, could only be experienced on a one-to-one basis.

In the mid '70s I was eager to embark on a new way of bookmaking. While many of my peers bound books in full leather with gold tooling and colorful onlays, these so-called designer bindings did not really grab me. Despite their impressive craftsmanship, I saw the books as rigid, compressed volumes with elaborate cover designs used as a focal point to readers to famous writers and titles. I much prefer making

a less inhibiting cover, a minimal gesture that helps readers gain access to the content rather than having them focus on a work of self-glorification.

As an artist, I see that the book is capable of transformation if taken out of conventional context. By not emphasizing its utilitarian function, the book can stand on its own without losing the thread of its historical past and set the stage for a different kind of reading experience.

In the process of finding my own mode of expression, I was drawn toward artists who approached the book as an object unencumbered by traditional boundaries. They showed me that though the book is a medium with certain rigid characteristics, it can be released from its confinement and become the perfect venue for presenting thought-provoking concepts. How I once typically defined a book no longer applied.

But I also found that I couldn't jump over my own shadow. My background in conservation took hold. I found that above all, I was interested in exploring the structure of the book. There was no escape. I became obsessed with the deconstruction of traditional examples, and with figuring out ways to reconstruct the components and devise new arrangements. Although

Oxbow Duo, 1997.
9 x 6 x ¼ inches
(22.9 x 15.2 x .6 cm).
Paper made by the artist; pulp with painted and stenciled images, one-sheet folded books format.
Photo by Paul Warchol.

Bug Book, 1999.
8½ x 5½ x ¾ inches
(21.6 x 14 x 1.9 cm).
Plastic, Mylar, Tyvek;
Gocco printed,
photocopied and
stamped images,
codex format.
Photo by Paul Warchol.

the book as a mechanical device is basically immune
to improvement, it is not immune to change.

Uppermost in my mind were the fringe-area formats—known as a cataloguer's nightmare because they
did not fit the norm. You can find these inspiring oddi-
ties in many libraries, assuming they were given a
chance to survive. I am talking about little known historical book structures like the *vade mecum* and the
hornbook, or one-of-a-kind innovations created by
individuals for a specific purpose. There are also books
from other cultures with pages made from tree bark,
palm leaves, bamboo, wood, or fabric. Their binding
techniques or packaging devices, and their mystifying
contents offer endless sources for inspiration.

I was also drawn to Japanese books with their airy,
lightweight, elegant, discreet covers, and superb
placement of text and images. The accordion book
especially cast a spell on me. Its simple method of
alternating mountain and valley folds could be
adapted to create gussets, hinges, spines, pop-ups and
fold-outs. Exploring this book and getting hold of its
mechanical ingenuity—its inherent magic—is still my
passion.

Since book conservation involves careful planning
and execution of tested methods, I prefer to work less
restrictively as a book artist. I want free time to exper-

iment to my heart's content, as if anything can happen,
and the outcome doesn't really matter. Combining
characteristic features of scroll, accordion book, and
codex, I come up with hybrids between tradition and
innovation. Sometimes these concoctions don't work,
but they still lead me to the next station.

By approaching my work this way, I have found
several key factors that influence my constructions.
One is that the book acts as a continuous structure
when individual elements share the distribution of
movement and stress. Another is the connection
between covers and pages, and between the pages
themselves, are the weakest points. I've learned that
the cooperation of materials plays an important part,
and is necessary to assure flawless action. Also, durability becomes essential when a book's function depends
on interaction and manipulation, when a book is nei-
ther static nor self-animated; the viewer as facilitator
may not understand a book's fragility and can con-
tribute to a dilemma when the book is handled.

My experimentation leads me to research materials
to learn about their properties and test their performance. While acid-free papers and boards guarantee
longevity, they tend to look bland and generic. In my
personal work I pay less attention to archival quality.
Instead I look for materials that have strength, texture,

and the endurance for folding. But I don't rule out less substantial materials. To the contrary, anything that arouses my curiosity has a good chance of ending up in my studio and becoming part of a book.

Inspiration for my imagery comes mostly from unexpected sources. I collect stuff that is normally regarded as debris. To me there is something miraculous about these scraps. Linked with other elements in a new arrangement, they become part of a visual, poetic narrative. Absurd out-of-place objects, illogical displays, organized chaos, or obsessive collections stimulate my imagination as much as the microscopically seen grain of sand or the ingenuous seedpod found in nature. I also draw ideas from the world of architecture and science, and from writing systems that are unintelligible to me.

Making a one-of-a-kind book involves many considerations that lead to envisioning the whole process. I see each book as an environment that sets the stage, so to speak, for an intimate journey. I want the viewer to enjoy a moment of playfulness and amusement, of bedazzlement and investigation. As I allow an interplay between structure and materials, I can imagine a toy, a machine, a bag, or a building. The book, being its own unique self, can also pose in disguise. Techniques such as printing, stenciling, rubbing, and stitching transport the content onto the page.

My books come slowly to completion. As pages expand, cutouts filter light, and shadows hush along, words and images wax and wane through transparent layers, and assemblages of fragments nestle in recesses. In the end, structure, materials, and content have to strike a lucky balance.

My approach to making book models is more spontaneous. This is one aspect of my work where the structure takes the front seat and the content is incidental, even removable or replaceable. These model books are often utilitarian, meant as depositories for preexisting portable collections and substances of all sorts, or they are prototypes for small editions. They speak of my engineering impulse and demonstrate a connection between books and buildings.

I am fascinated when I discover that certain rhythms and relationships between interacting parts are based on mathematical principles. Finally, there comes the notion that the laws of proportion and

order can be a stimulant rather than drudgery. Often I am stuck with a three-dimensional doodle that seems to lead nowhere. But like the intensity of a toothache, it won't let me rest. Totally preoccupied, I test and probe before, finally, a new prototype materializes.

My models are the foundation for the many workshops I lead; not so much to claim invention, but rather to inspire and entice students to rediscover the book for themselves. In trying to materialize my ideas, I find problems to solve and techniques to devise. As the teacher, I am concerned with procedures that should, at best, follow a logical order. I have to know the steps and understand their pitfalls first. Then, since pitfalls always serve us well in learning, I need to provide the opportunity for students to find the pitfalls themselves so they can learn that they can fix them. My spirit is lifted when something finally clicks and I can welcome a new model for a future workshop.

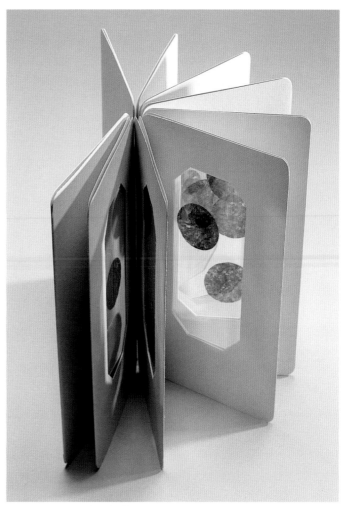

Storage Book, 1999. 7½ x 4½ x ¾ inches (19 x 11.4 x 1.9 cm). Library board, Mylar, seaweed circles; folded pages attached to a concertina spine. *Photo by Paul Warchol.*

Certain Sensation, 2002. 7 x 4½ x ⅜ inches (17.8 x 11.4 x .95 cm). Handmade paper; Gocco printed and collaged images, expendable page construction format. *Photo by Paul Warchol.*

The process of making a book is often more exhilarating than seeing the finished product. We have become alienated from the notion that the objects of one's desire can be made by hand. Children and adults are thrilled to learn they can make books on their own without expensive tools or the need for a special space. In fact, some of the best books have been made at the kitchen table.

A pair of hands and a bone folder alone can transform a single sheet of paper into connecting pages and covers. There are many ways to do so. Trying again and again means you learn about proportions and the versatility of the fold. The concertina fold best demonstrates the effect of opposite directions in regard to mountain and valley folds. Use it as a point of departure, as a modus operandi for single-sheetbooks, folders, and rows of pockets. You will be surprised what is on the horizon—perhaps something that you can hardly imagine as a descendant of the venerable book.

On the day of the blizzard in 1996 in Philadelphia, the snow piled up high in the streets and the traffic stopped dead. Nobody went to work. It was all white and quiet. A perfect day to spend in the studio. I cut long strips of paper and began folding them in concertina fashion. Soon several neat rectangular stacks were lying on my workbench.

The next procedure involved creasing and reversing the corners at different angles to the vertical fold. Finally triangles were folded back on themselves. This resulted in rows of pockets with narrow or wide gussets depending on the radius of the angle.

Eventually—the day was almost gone—it occurred to me to make the corner meet the middle fold, and form a right angle. It was quite a thrill to realize that the whole thing was now upside down and the gussets no longer extended the pockets. Instead they connected pages in a unique way. The book had more or less bound itself. Several months later there was talk of the birth of "blizzard babies," those conceived during the snowstorm. That's when I began to call the outcome of my folding adventure the *Blizzard Book*.

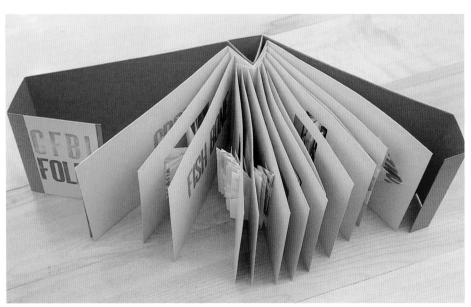

CFBL Folds, 2003. 8 x 10 x 2½ inches (20.3 x 25.4 x 6.4 cm). Aquaba paper, various papers from the French Paper Company, folded objects; letterpress and Gocco printing, structure designed to hold three-dimensional objects. *Photo by Paul Warchol.*

HEDI KYLE

Hands On

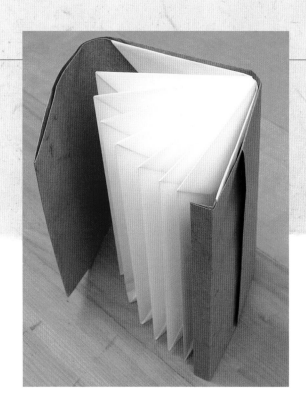

Made from one strip of paper and using no adhesives or sewing techniques to link the pages, the Blizzard Book has pages that are like pockets. This allows for diverse content that can be removed or replaced, making the book suggestive to adaptations. Hedi first demonstrates the techniques for making her Blizzard Book, and then makes a cover for it. Included are Hedi's illustrations that act as folding diagrams.

Folded Structures

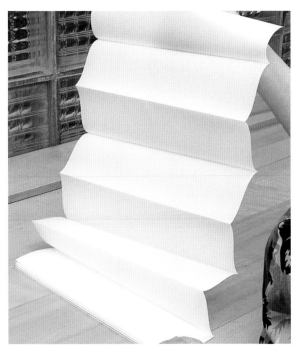

1. The initial folds produce a strip of paper with 16 equal concertina folds. The strip shown here measures 15 x 6 inches (37.5 x 165 cm). This is drawing vellum, but I also recommend Tyvek or Elephant Hide paper.

2. The next step is to fold the corners of each of the concertina folds by lining up the corners with the center crease.

3. Using a bone folder to flatten the diagonal creases, I fold all the corners of the double panels.

5. In preparation for making the reverse folds in the next step, the triangles are unfolded.

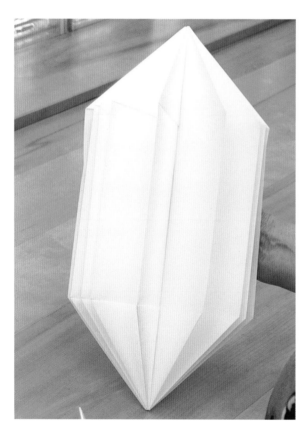

4. The resulting form.

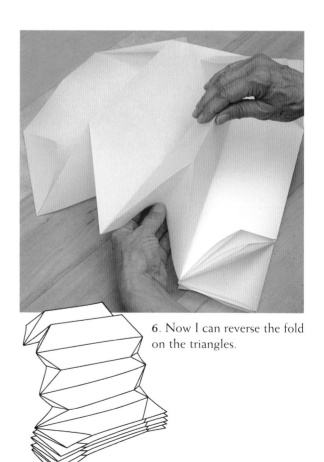

6. Now I can reverse the fold on the triangles.

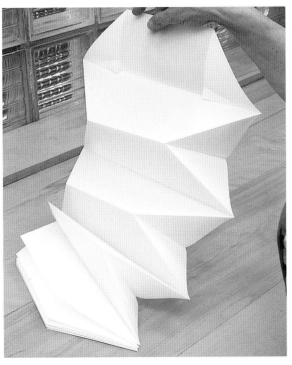

7. This is the form with the triangles reverse-folded.

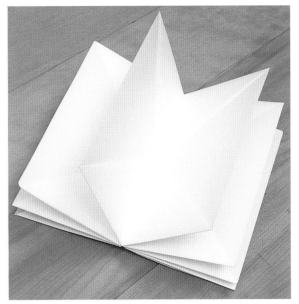

9. The finished book

8. The large triangles that I made from the reverse folds are folded into the center crease. You can see how one will overlap the other to form the pockets of the book.

10. Here is a detail of the spine showing how the pages connect.

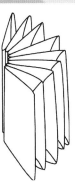

Variable Proportions for the Blizzard Book

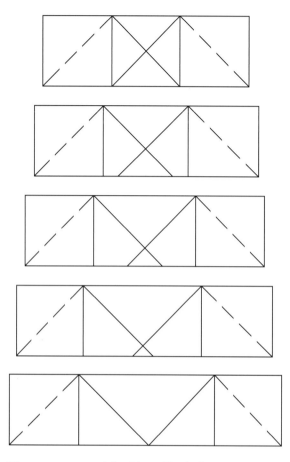

The proportions of the *Blizzard Book* change based on the desired size for the finished book. The size options range between using a strip that is the length of three squares to one that is the length of four squares as shown above. One square must remain at each end. The page can be square or rectangular as long as the total length of the strip does not exceed the measurement of four squares. When it does exceed the measurement, the folded triangles will not meet or overlap to form the pockets.

The Cover

To prepare, I make two jigs, A and B, and one spine piece. Jig A is the height of the page of the *Blizzard Book* plus $\frac{1}{16}$ inch (.15 cm) by the width of the page plus $\frac{9}{16}$ inch (1.5 cm). Jig B is the height of the page plus $\frac{1}{16}$ inch by the width of the page plus $\frac{1}{16}$ inch. The spine piece is the height of the page plus $\frac{1}{16}$ inch by the thickness of all pages, in this example $\frac{1}{2}$ inch (1.3 cm). Using Elephant Hide paper, I cut the strip for the cover to these dimensions:

Height = 2 x the height of jig A
Length = 3 x the width of jig A +
1 spine thickness + 4 x the width of jig B

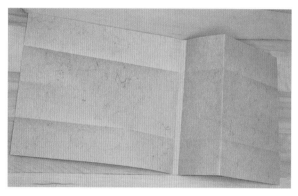

11. This is the strip after making the first folds. They were made by first marking the height of jig A on both short sides of the strip, folding the long sides to meet these marks, then unfolding the long sides. Next, starting at the right side, three widths of jig A and one spine thickness were marked. Finally, the spine folds and another fold that is one width of jig A away from the spine fold were made.

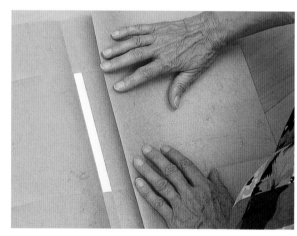

12. After gluing the spine strip in place, I make a pleat by folding width A adjacent to the spine in half. The pleat will later serve as a pocket to hold the cover flap in place.

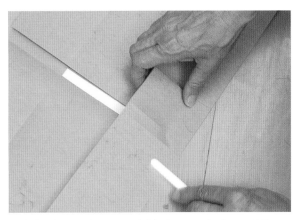

13. The long sides are refolded towards the middle, and the right cover portion is doubled to meet the spine.

14. A ½-inch (1.3 cm) yap edge serves as a break between the inner portion of the cover that will be tucked into the last page and the outer portion. A ½-inch strip of brass and a bone folder are used to score the yap edge.

15. The yap edge is flattened.

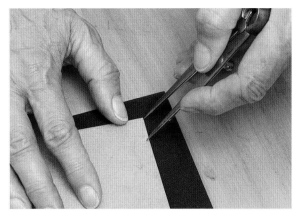

16. The sides of the inner cover portion need to be angled for a better fit when inserting the page. To make the angles, I open the cover and mark the inner edge ¾ inch (1.9 cm) away from the top and bottom. Following these marks, diagonal creases are made to the first yap fold.

17. Then I reverse fold the diagonal creases made in step 16.

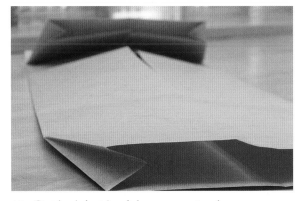

18. On the left side of the cover strip, the reverse-folded diagonal creases are repeated. I start the creases at the ¾-inch (1.9 cm) marks at the edge and end one width of jig B away. Here you can see the completed creases on the left part of the cover strip.

19. To attach the cover, the first and last pages of the *Blizzard Book* are inserted into the two angled portions of the cover.

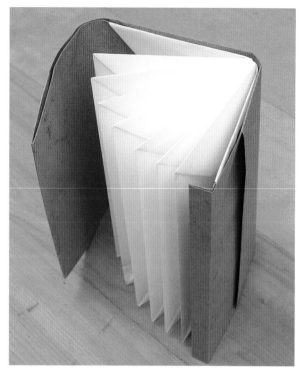

20. This shows the finished cover with book. Notice the pocket on the right cover that was created by the pleat made in step 12. As a finishing touch, and for a better fit, the left flap was angled and reverse-folded. It can then be slid into the pocket.

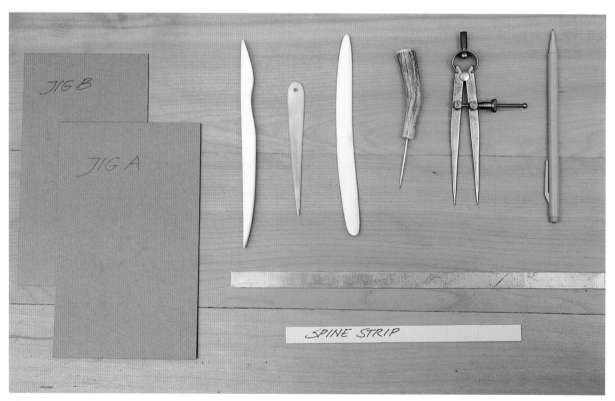

The jigs and tools for making the cover.

About the Artist

HEDI KYLE recently retired from her position as head conservator at the American Philosophical Society. She continues to instruct students in the field of book arts at The University of the Arts in Philadelphia. Conservation and traditional bookmaking have served as a frame of reference for her teaching and personal work. Her inventive, one-of-a-kind constructions have been exhibited internationally and are in numerous private and public collections. She is renowned for her folded structures. She is a co-founder of the Paper and Book Intensive, and has given workshops in the USA, Canada, and Europe.

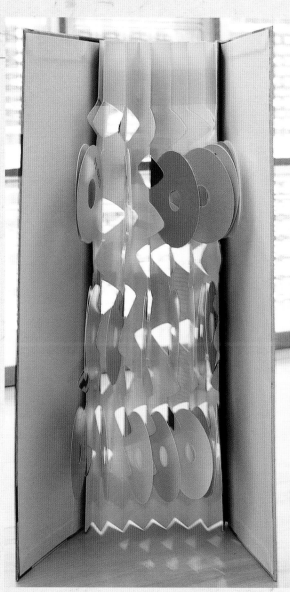

Rattlepeek, 2003. 11 x 3½ x ½ inches (27.9 x 8.9 x 1.3 cm). Reeves paper; board; found discs; color-copied images on covers and reverse concertina; flagbook format. *Photo by Paul Warchol.*

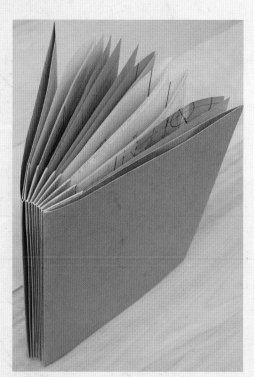

Crown Book, 2003. 7½ x 5¾ inches (18.8 x 14.5 cm). Aquaba and Elephant Hide papers. *Blizzard Book* format. *Photo by Paul Warchol.*

Detail of *Crown Book.*

Gallery

The eight book artists selected for this gallery are special to me for different reasons. Over the past 25 years I have been inspired by their work, followed their careers, and touched base on occasion.

From the moment I met Barbara Mauriello when she was a young apprentice at The Center for Book Arts in New York city, I fell under the spell of her lighthearted spirit. Her work, a vibrant interplay of color, form, and surface, stimulates joy. Pamela Spitzmueller, book conservator and book artist, juxtaposes not only the traditional and the experimental, but the innovative and mundane. Her dry humor and her offbeat use of materials make her work irresistible to me.

If one person can infuse me with awe, it is Claire Van Vliet. Committed to her Janus Press for 50 years, she has advanced the approach to bookmaking and is truly a master of her trade. For a long time I have admired Keith Smith and Scott McCarney, one an investigator of intricate book structures, the other an inventor of fantastic book forms.

Carol Barton, with her long-time focus on pop-up books, is an expert on devising methods for their construction. I am intrigued with her work, because it is intelligent, simplified, and well planned. Emily Martin's books bear a strong imprint of their maker, and I like them for being straightforward and not pretentious. Her personal stories, short and poignant, become universal.

Bill Drendel delights in funny factuality and creates fantastic and unusual book objects. He challenges the perception of what a book is supposed to be. I love his unrestrained approach to making books. As book conservator and book artist, Denise Carbone pursues traditional techniques, relishes experiments, and delights to provoke through subject matter. I find her work very exciting and stimulating.

Emily Martin, *The Vicious Circle Series,* 1997. 4 x 4 x 2 inches (10.2 x 10.2 x 5 cm) each.
Set of five stacking and rotating rings with circular text; letterpress printed on handmade flax paper. *Photo by Meryl Marek.*

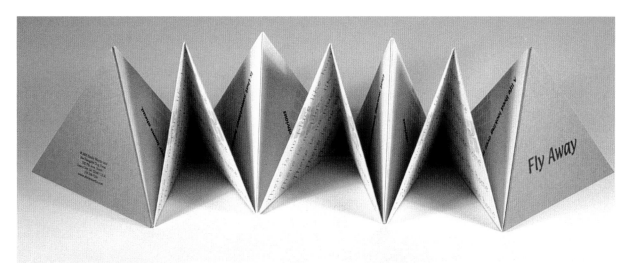

Emily Martin, *Fly Away*, 2003. Closed: 8 x 6 x 1 inches (20.3 x 15.2 x 2.5 cm); Open: 8 x 6 x 26 inches (20.3 x 15.2 x 66 cm). Pouchoir and archival inkjet on Sakamoto paper; nontraditional variation of double-leaved accordion with attached hard cover wrapped in Moriki paper. *Photo by Meryl Marek.*

Emily Martin, *My Twelve Steps*, 1997. Closed: 6 x 6 x 1 inches (15.2 x 15.2 x 2.5 cm); Open: 6 x 6 x 6 inches (15.2 x 15.2 x 15.2 cm). Letterpress printed on Rives heavyweight paper; case bound with flax and Moriki paper over acid-free binders board, bamboo and cotton pull cord with bead stops for the closing. *Photo by Meryl Marek.*

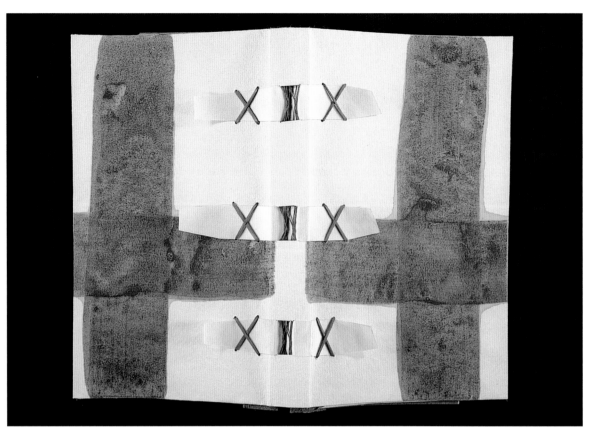

Denise Carbone, *Y Z X ? Æ,* 2000. 12 x 7.5 x 1 inches (metrics). Pages: paper, homemade ink, rubbing, press type, found object, white out, photocopy; cover: flax paper, homemade ink. *Photo by Frank Margeson.*

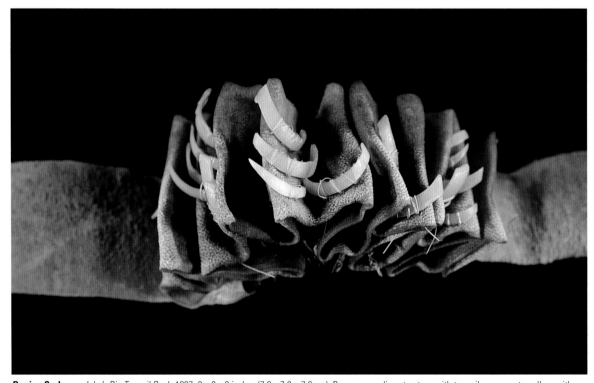

Denise Carbone, *Jake's Big Toenail Book,* 1997. 3 x 3 x 3 inches (7.6 x 7.6 x 7.6 cm). Pages: accordion structure with toenails sewn onto vellum with horsehair; cover: pigskin soaked in liquid and left to dry. *Photo by Frank Margeson.*

HEDI KYLE

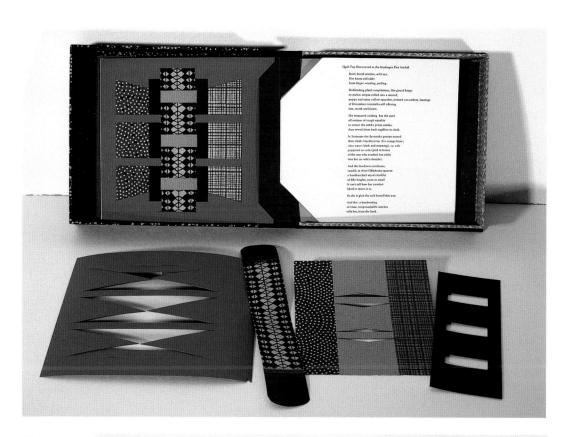

Claire Van Vliet, *Beauty in Use,* by Sandra McPherson, 1997. 9 x 8 inches (22.9 x 20.3 cm). Cut papers; letterpress printed.

Photo by John Somers.

Pamela Spitzmueller, *Homage to Walt Whitman*, 1994. Closed: 8 x 10 x 2 inches (20.3 x 25.4 x 5 cm); Open: 48 x 66 x 8 inches (122 x 167.6 x 20.3 cm). Stencil; photocopy; acrylic paint; vintage and modern papers; ink; Whitman poem written in ink on board surfaces. *Photo by the artist.*

Barbara Mauriello, *Parchment People*, 2002.4½ x 4 x 1inches (11.4 x 10.2 x 2.5 cm). 18th Century parchment, plastic buttons, linen thread, handmade paper. *Photos by Raffi/Van Chromes.*

Scott McCarney, Untitled (Pedestal Book), 1981. 9 x 9 x 4 inches (22.9 x 22.9 x 10.2 cm). Black and colored Canson Mi-teintes papers bound in a flag-book concertina style on four sides; board case covered in English marble and Japanese rice papers with attached cross-structure legs. *Photo by the artist.*

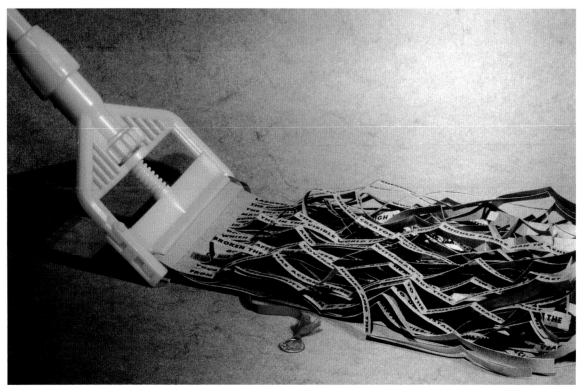

William Drendel, *Laborem Exercens (John Paul XXIII Encyclical on the Dignity of Human Work)*, 1997. 6½ x 74 x 3 inches (16.5 x 188 x 7.6 cm). Mop handle; laser-printed text on Elephant Hide paper. *Photo by the artist.*

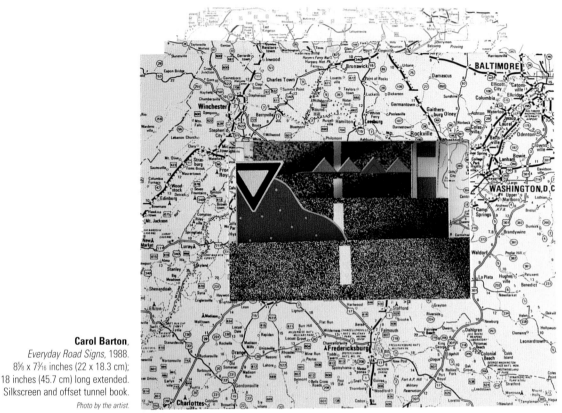

Carol Barton,
Everyday Road Signs, 1988.
8⅝ x 7³⁄₁₆ inches (22 x 18.3 cm);
18 inches (45.7 cm) long extended.
Silkscreen and offset tunnel book.
Photo by the artist.

Scott McCarney, *Alphabook I*, 1981. 4¾ x 6½ inches (12 x 16.5 cm). Hand-cut gray/cream duplex stock, folded and glued into board covers decorated with printer's make-ready.
Photo by the artist.

Emily Martin, *Eight Slices of Pie*, 2002. 9 inches (22.9 cm) diameter. Inkjet printed on text paper with purchased aluminum pie tin and plastic cover.
Photo by Meryl Marek.

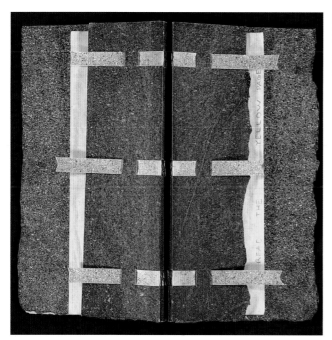

Denise Carbone, *Yellow Pages*, 1997.
Closed: 4½ x 9 inches (11.4 x 22.9 cm); Open: 9 x 9 inches (22.9 x 22.9 cm).
Text: yellow theme paper, photocopy transfer, white-out, rubbings;
cover: sprinkled gouache on flax paper, vellum tapes, silk suture thread.
Photos by Frank Margeson.

Barbara Mauriello

*I*n her work as a bookbinder, Barbara
Mauriello makes boxes as protective
containers for rare books. As a book artist,
she turns the boxes inside out to expose the
heart of the narrative. Readers who
encounter her boxes are delighted to
discover that the outside of a book can
be as compelling as the inside.

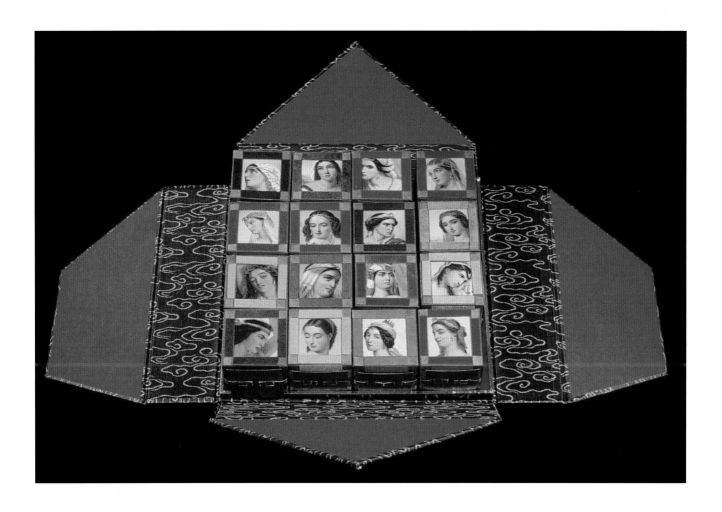

Women of the Bible: From Abigail to Queen of Sheba, 1985. 9¼ x 9½ x 2½ (23 x 23.8 x 6.25 cm). Salvaged 18th-century illustrated book, dyed Japanese tissue, card stock, bookcloth over boards, pewter clasp. *Photo by Richard Minsky.*

Boxes, Inside Out

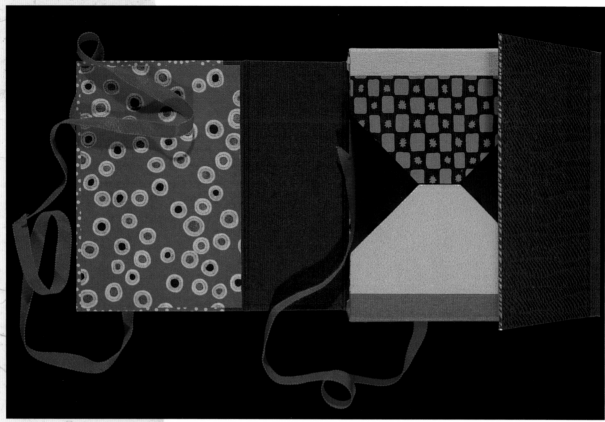

Patchwork Box, 1999.
6½ x 5¾ x 2 ¾ inches
(16.2 x 14.4 x 7 cm).
Japanese printed
papers, bookcloth,
ribbon. *Photo by Raffi/*
Van Chromes.

Almost 25 years ago, at the urging from my reading of Virginia Woolf, I walked into The Center for Book Arts, a tiny storefront on Bleecker Street near The Bowery in New York City. I'd been reading everything by and about this great writer, and was intrigued to learn that she and her husband started setting type and printing their own Hogarth Press publications partly to soothe Virginia's frazzled nerves which erupted upon completion of her novels.

I soon discovered that setting type by hand had the exact opposite effect on me; it actually induced migraines—all those tiny bits of metal upside down and backwards in the wrong drawers. I decided to get out of the type shop. But it was too late! I was drawn into the bindery by bowls of warm, (it was freezing in the downstairs type shop) freshly cooked paste, and those glorious paste brushes. And that's where I've stayed ever since.

Among my first teachers was Richard Minsky-in-absentia: he was in England on a fellowship during the first year of my apprenticeship, but I heard all the sto-ries of this Book Arts eccentric, and I do believe that even then—and certainly in the years since I've actually gotten to know him—I was the beneficiary of his zany brilliance. He always asked the important questions like, "Why are you *praying* over that book in the press, when you should actually be *looking* at it, whereupon you will see that you are smashing its spine?" It was also as an apprentice that I studied with Hedi Kyle, whose manipulation of a sheet of paper can only be called magic.

As a bookbinder, I made boxes as protective containers for books. But I began to see boxes as more. Like books, they too are objects of mystery and delight. They hide our secrets. They protect our family stories. They may even have saved a life or two, if the small beauty pictured on the next page—an 18th century tarot card box disguised as a book—did its job. Even empty boxes seduce us with their startling typography, fancy closures, dynamic paper engineering, and evocative scents. In the history of movies,

BARBARA MAURIELLO

Tarot Card Box, poss. Germany 18th century. 5½ x 3¼ x 1½ inches (13.8 x 8 x 3.8 cm). Pasteboard, marbled and paste-painted papers, leather. From the collection of The Center for Book Arts. *Photo by Raffi/Van Chromes.*

there is no image more poignant than Jem's cigar box in *To Kill A Mockingbird,* in which the history of the strange man and saviour Boo Radley is both hidden and revealed. I make boxes almost every day. When I close the lid and send a box on its way, I know that its life has just begun.

My fascination with boxes started in the kitchen pantry of my childhood. The first box I fell in love with was a Quaker Oats cereal box, that enticing, round canister with the high-hatted gentleman smiling out at the world. My sisters and I punched holes in the lids and bottoms, threaded string from one end to the other, and wore our "drums" around our necks. And who could resist the vibrant red-and-yellow tins of Davis Baking Powder? Those same boxes, decades later, greet me in my studio—the oat boxes hold buttons, and the tins, now filled with pennies, serve as bookbinding weights.

Today I am more likely to be inspired at a flea market than in the grocery store. In addition to the thrill of the physical object, flea-market finds have the emotional tug of the lost or forgotten lives that inhabited these objects. A Sunday walk through the 26th Street Flea Market in New York might turn up treasures, but there is also a certain sadness in the shoeboxes of discarded photographs, and the mountains of postcards with their messages ranging from the tender, "My Dear Angel Win, Was dreaming and thinking of you all night...," to the mundane, "Walter, Don't forget to take out the garbage tomorrow night. Mother."

A tracing of thread, or a bit of handwriting, confirm that a fragment of a life is as captivating as a fully told story. I gather up the photos, recreate families in the pages of new albums, box the postcards, and sort the buttons. It's the least I can do for these generous, anonymous donors to my art.

I am lucky to live across the river from New York City. A recent walk through Chinatown led me to sheets of brilliantly block-printed Tibetan papers priced less than a newspaper. That same day, my favorite art-supply store was selling vintage Japanese printed papers at bargain prices; I bought an armful. I've found Betty Boop buttons from the 1930s in a carton of junk on Canal Street, and 18th-century indentured servant documents—mightily mouse-eaten—in a trunk on 26th Street. The best moment is when I return home, spread out my treasures, and go to work. Since I spend a good part of my life working on commissioned projects over which I don't have total design control, it is thrilling to select and discard materials at will, without consulting others, and without knowing quite how things will turn out.

My students are another source of both inspiration and raw ingredients. The poets in my classes pose

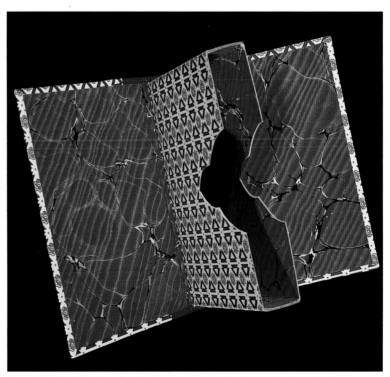

Tarot Card, 2001. 6½ x 4¼ x 1½ inches (16.2 x 10.6 x 3.8 cm). Museum board, card stock, hand-marbled and English printed papers, leather; scored-paper box nestled inside of a rounded case. *Photo by Raffi/Van Chromes.*

different dilemmas than the photographers. Painters and printmakers demand structures bypassed by makers of computer-generated art. Readers just want to save their beloved books. Their questions send me back to my workbench to develop or refine models, or to investigate new materials. Along the way I am offered delicious tidbits: a tin of buttons, a bundle of cards, a carved wooden stamp. One day a student handed me a plastic bag filled with the burnt and soggy remnants of an 18th-century illustrated book, a victim of a fire, and said, "Here, you'll like this." I did. My reconstruction of those beautiful fragments became *Women of the Bible: From Abigail to the Queen of Sheba.*

Among artists, I am most in love with the bold painters of the early 20th century: Sonia Delaunay

and Liubov Popova for their brilliant use of color; Matisse for his brazen paper cut-outs; Paul Klee and Wassily Kandinsky for their kinetic geometric abstractions. Moroccan tiles, Japanese textiles, Brazilian folk art, Islamic calligraphy—everywhere I look, there is something to delight the eye and to take back to the studio.

I found this little wooden box (left and below) in a flea market in France. It charmed me with its painting and triptych-like structure, and inspired my Hands On section for this book. The mechanics of its pivoting doors, closing with a wonderful clattering noise, intrigued me even more. I've used the bookbinder's skills, tools, and vocabulary to translate its parts into a box whose story is told both inside and out.

Making my first prototype is all about construction. In recreating a found object, I name the parts of the original object as closely as possible to the language of the book: head, tail, spine, and fore-edge. I find this especially important from a teaching point of view to give students a familiar reference. Then, I analyze the object for its construction details and substitute known materials for the unknown, in this case paper, book board, and parchment for the wood.

On the flea market box, I noticed how uncomplicated the closure was. Interpreted in my materials, I figured a simple strip of covered book board glued onto one door would closely replicate this feature. I had to decide if I was going to line the doors with raised panels, or with a single layer of paper because I knew this

Flea-Market Box, India, 20th century. 5½ x 7 x 1¼ inches (13.8 x17.5 x 3.1cm). Painted wood. From the collection of Barbara Mauriello.
Photo by Raffi/Van Chromes.

decision would affect the depth of the box. I considered mounting the main panel flush to the baseboard, but decided to make it float instead, which would also affect the depth of the tray. Other options I considered were adding feet to the box to make it more like furniture—a true cabinet of curiosities—and whether I should manipulate photographs in some form of accordion fold or tunnel-book format to make the photographs the subject of the box.

Once I have a working model, I go to town on the materials—and that is where joy enters the project. My *Triptych Box* is deceptively close to the commonest of four-walled trays—the base of box making. It's the uncommon use of materials, and those pivoting doors, which transform the box. When I started this project, my goals were twofold: first, figure out a door-opening mechanism; and second, make the box's content interesting enough to bother opening the doors. Later developments, like stencilling on the parchment and gold tooling on the doors, seemed to spring out on their own. Having a technical problem to solve gives me a concrete focal point at the outset of a project; later the words and pictures fly around the workbench, some to be caught, some to escape.

When I cut out the boards for a four-walled tray, I must judge the height, width, and depth of the box by its contents. The starting point is, at the same time, the ending point. The painted parchment panel floating on the base of my box, and the two smaller panels lining the doors, define the three dimensions of the tray. After the tray is assembled and covered, I have all the information I need to proceed to the outermost parts of the box, in this case its doors, its roof, and its floor—I like stealing architectural terms and applying them to boxes which are, ultimately, houses for books or other objects.

As someone with a disastrous history in mathematics, I have developed a system of measuring without numbers. Numbers are too abstract. They exist as lines on a ruler, and it's easy to pick the wrong line, or even the wrong ruler! My method is to consider the specifics of the project—the particular thickness of the boards and the covering materials and the relationship of one element to another—and to take continuous "readings" directly from these components as the book or box is being built. This means that I cannot cut out all of the

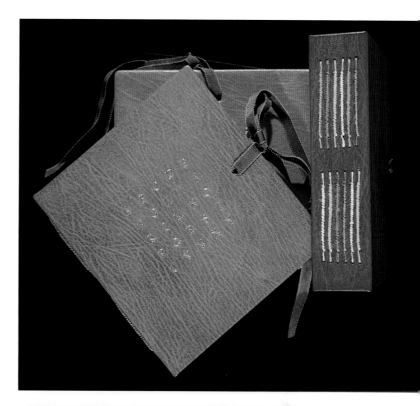

Alphabet Books, 2000. 5 x 4¾ x 1¾ inches (12.5 x 12 x 4.4 cm). Tacket bindings; leather with linen tackets, gold tooling, ribbon ties. *Photo by Raffi/Van Chromes.*

parts in advance which, I admit, might slow down the construction process.

However, it's a habit of mine to cut all materials that share the same measurements at the same time—even if some of these pieces don't show up until much later in

BARBARA MAURIELLO

Painted Parchment Purses, 2003. 4½ x 7 x 2 inches (11.3 x 17.5 x 5 cm). Pochoir on 18th century-parchment; handmade paper, vintage buttons, leather straps. *Photo by Raffi/Van Chromes.*

a project. For example, once my tray is glued, but before it's covered, I cut out a board to the height of the tray and put it aside. This is the board from which I will, in a later step, cut my doors.

My approach lets the box grow organically into a lively creature on the workbench, with every part getting its start from the previously cut piece. For example,

if I were measuring the thickness of a deck of cards, I would crease a scrap of paper to create a right angle and slide the paper under the deck, snugly enclosing the cards within this right angle. I would then make a parallel sharp crease in this paper, over the upper surface of the deck of cards, and voila! Captured on this little scrap, between two creases, is the true thickness of my cards. I now place this valuable scrap on my board and mark for cutting.

If I need a board equal to the thickness of my deck of cards plus two board thicknesses, then I literally pick up two scraps of board, add them to my scrap-paper measure, mark, and cut. You will see in the Hands On section how I employ this method using a length of thread and a scrap of paper to cut my tray-covering paper to the proper dimensions. Since my favorite polka-dot paper is available in an unusually small sheet size, you will also notice that I need to piece two strips together in order to wrap my tray.

Regarding adhesives, every bookbinder has her favorite recipes. Mine include paste, glue, and methyl-cellulose. The adhesive with the most grab is glue; I use PVA (polyvinyl acetate) when I need immediate, quick-bonding action—as in assembling the tray of the box.

When I need more working time, especially when handling stubborn materials, I turn to either paste or a mixture of glue and methyl cellulose. Experience will tell you which bowl to dip your brush into. The only rule I compulsively follow is the one that tells me that, when working with paper, the adhesive is applied to the paper. If you place a dry paper on a wet board, the paper will attempt to stretch and will wrinkle.

Boxes, like books, start inside out—you can't begin to build either until you know what's at their heart. Having made hundreds of rare-book boxes in my years as a book conservator—sturdy, dull boxes hiding the most astonishing books—I wanted the box itself to astonish, and not to be a mere container. My standards for boxes are simple: if the viewer opens the box immediately, then the box is probably a failure.

House of Cards, 2000. 6 x 6 x 4 inches (15 x 15 x 10 cm). Vintage postcards; embroidery. *Photo by Raffi/Van Chromes.*

Hands On

The inspiration for Barbara's Triptych Box comes from a flea-market find (see page 142). Here she demonstrates how she departs from four-walled tray construction to create an expressive work.

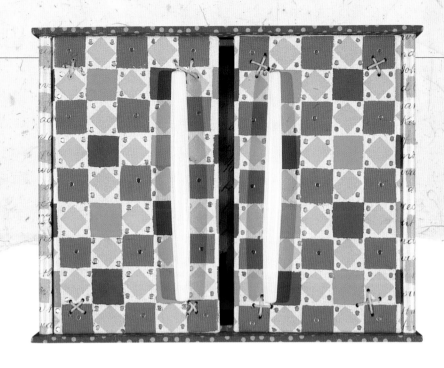

Box Construction

1. The stencils, paints, handle tools, decorative paper, and parchment for making the box.

2. I begin by cutting out the tray at the board cutter.

3. The walls are glued onto the tray. Here I'm gluing on the fourth wall.

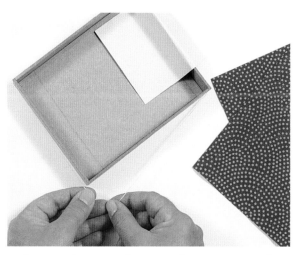

4. A piece of string and a scrap of paper serve as the tools for measuring the tray for its covering papers.

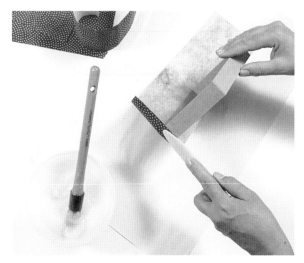

5. After placing the tray on the pasted decorative paper, I wrap the tray and smooth the paper with a bone folder.

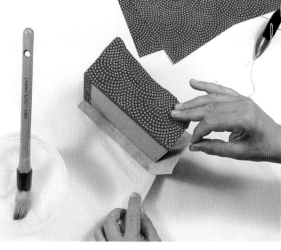

6. The partially wrapped tray is rolled onto a second sheet of the pasted decorative paper.

7. With a triangle as the straightedge, a knife makes the cuts for turning the paper to the inside of the tray.

8. Here I'm pasting the final turn-in.

9. The doors are covered after cutting the corners of the paper before turning in.

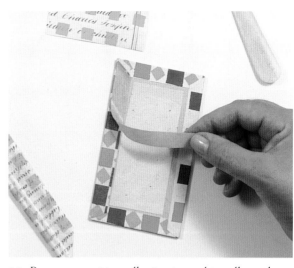

12. Pressure-sensitive adhesive is used to adhere the hinges.

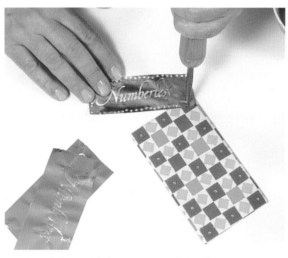

10. I tool the gold dots on one of the doors.

13. I cover stock with the parchment manuscript to make the door liners.

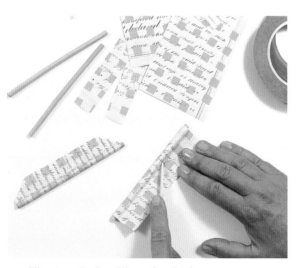

11. The dowels that I'll use for the hinges are wrapped. Afterwards, I cut the corners of the parchment for a neat application on the door.

14. Now it's time to do the stenciling on the door liners.

15. The bone handle is sewn onto a door.

16. Then the liner is adhered to the door.

17. After punching holes through the door and liner, decorative reinforcements are stitched through the lining panel.

18. Using decorative paper, I cover what will become the "roof" and "floor" boards of the box.

19. In order to mark the placement for the dowel hinge, I position the floor but do not adhere it. The door is held in place while marking.

20. To accommodate the dowel hinges, holes are punched in the floor and roof.

BARBARA MAURIELLO

21. The tail wall of the tray is glued to adhere the floorboard to the tray.

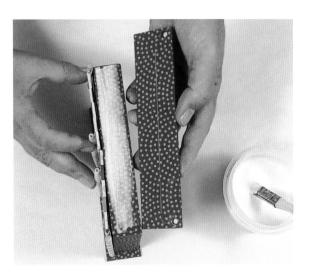

22. After inserting the dowel hinges into the floor holes made in step 20, I glue on the roof.

23. A painted panel covers the back of the box.

24. The last step is installing the artwork.

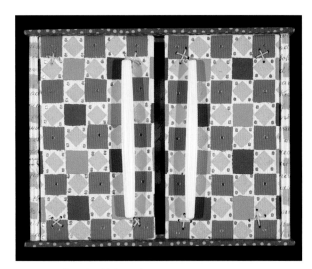

25. The finished *Triptych Box*

26. The pieces that make up the *Triptych Box*

BARBARA MAURIELLO

About the Artist

BARBARA MAURIELLO is an artist and conservator who has a bookbinding studio in Hoboken, New Jersey. She is on the faculty at the International Center for Photography and The Center for Book Arts. She conducts workshops at art centers across the country including Penland School of Crafts and Haystack Mountain School of Crafts. She has been an instructor at the Paper and Book Intensive, and the Cooper-Hewitt National Design Museum. In 2000, Barbara published the book *Making Memory Boxes* (Rockport Publishers).

The Triptych Box, 2003. 5½ x 7 x 1½ inches (13.8 x 17.5 x 3.8 cm). 18th-and 19th-century parchment, bone beads, Japanese printed paper, wooden dowels, linen thread, book board, museum board, hand-stenciled papers with gouache and gold tooling.
Photo by Raffi/Van Chromes.

Gallery

I owe everything to Richard Minsky who, 30 years ago, had the courage and the passion to create The Center for Book Arts. I walked into that crowded, cold little storefront and my life changed. Richard's books taught (and still teach) me that the binding must reflect the text—lessons beautifully reflected in both Sappho's Leap *and* Any Woman's Blues. *Richard also taught me how to look at books in the larger sense: to note historical links from one binding style to another, to pay attention to the book's physical weight (is it too much? too little? does it surprise?), and to ask the ultimate question, "Does the book resonate?" His most certainly do.*

I also credit Hedi Kyle—teacher, colleague, friend—for making me fall in love with bookbinding all those years ago. Whenever I look at her own miraculous books, I get the feeling that I am confronting dazzling new species within the insect community: pages fold, unfold, pivot, spin, dance, fly away, return. Dense with colors, words, and pictures, yet as light as air, Hedi's pages defy the laws of physics and celebrate the physicality of materials all at the same time. (Like I said, miraculous.) When I hear the word "slipcase" I think of the most ordinary of containers. But look at Hedi's charmer pictured here! It's functional, but so unexpectedly playful that its practicality is only subliminally revealed. The same is true of her Storage Book for 3-D Objects. It is simple, graceful, tantalyzing, beautiful.

Robert Warner, *ABC Window Boxes,* 2003. 4 x 4 x 6 inches (10.2 x 10.2 x 15.2 cm). Mixed media collage; box binding. *Photo by Louise Millmann.*

Pamela Spitzmueller, one of this country's top book conservators, is an artist in all that she does. Her curiosity about bookbinding in its strangest configurations has allowed her to take (figuratively!) treasures from the stacks of great libraries and re-invent them as small marvels of a 20th-century bookbinder's art. When you first look at her Preserved Book Series you think you're viewing an archeological relic. But then you note the materials—a Mason jar where you are expecting a clay jar—and the historical reference explodes. Humor, sleight-of-hand, superb craftsmanship, and scholarship are Pam's wonderful, and rare gifts.

I have said that as a teacher I am continually being taught by my students. Three days into a week-long workshop on boxmaking, I sidled up to one student, Robert Warner, and whispered into his ear, "Psst! Wanna teach a class with me?" Fortunately, he did, and this spiritual heir to Max Ernst and Joseph Cornell astonishes me with his quirky, surreal, tender constructions. Robert is famous for his Poet Boxes. One day a year he walks across the Brooklyn Bridge, Poet Box in hand, and poets (and regular people,too!) in tow, in celebration of poetry. Emily Dickinson has never been in better hands. I think that Robert and Virginia Woolf would have been great pals. He actually loves to set type, and he could have taught Virginia and Leonard a thing or two about letter spacing.

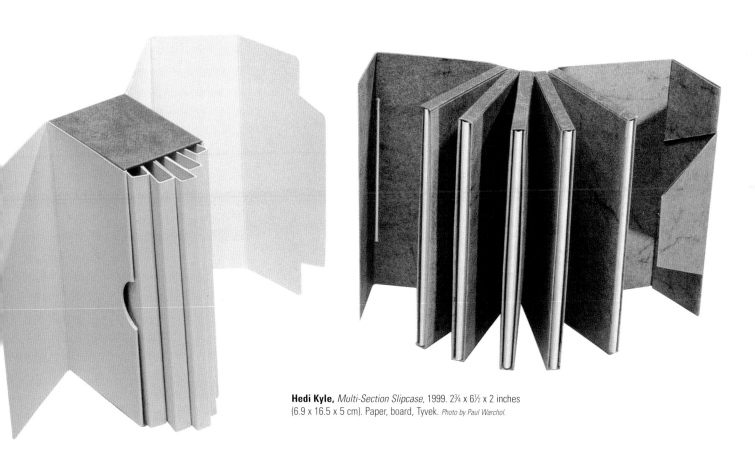

Hedi Kyle, *Multi-Section Slipcase,* 1999. 2¾ x 6½ x 2 inches (6.9 x 16.5 x 5 cm). Paper, board, Tyvek. *Photo by Paul Warchol.*

Pamela Spitzmueller, *Preserved Book Series, #14,*1992. 8 x 3 x 3 inches (20.3 x 7.6 x 7.6 cm). Sand, canning jar, traditional zinc metal lid; artificially aged and cockled papers (tinted with watercolors and fabric dyes) sewn through driftwood spine using long stitches.
Photo by the artist.

Pamela Spitzmueller, *Personal Devotional,* 1998. 8 x 14 x 4 inches (20.3 x 35.6 x 10.2 cm). Paper folded and sewn onto raised supports laced and pegged into boards; silk envelope pockets attach book boards to velvet over cover; corners weighted with tassels concealing lead fishing weights; repetitive text written across gutters and around facing pages; small leather buttons pasted to text block edge for page markers. *Photo by the artist.*

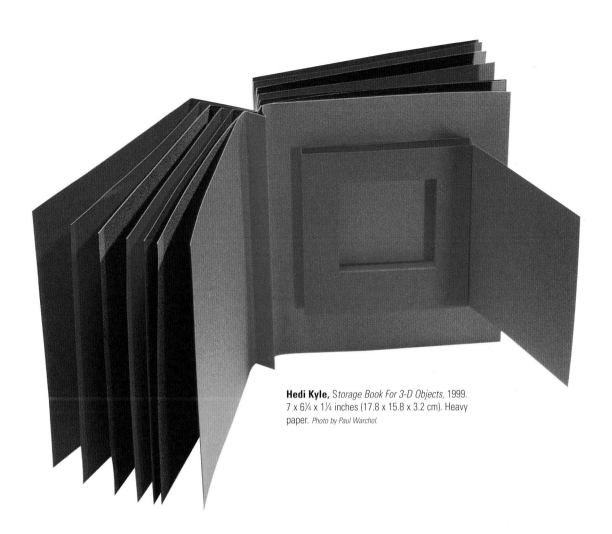

Hedi Kyle, *Storage Book For 3-D Objects,* 1999.
7 x 6¼ x 1¼ inches (17.8 x 15.8 x 3.2 cm). Heavy
paper. *Photo by Paul Warchol.*

Robert Warner, *Emily Dickinson, Hope & Snake,* 2003. 10 x 4½ x 2½ inches (25.4 x 11.4 x 6.4 cm). Mixed media collage; letterpress printed. *Photo by Louise Millmann.*

Richard Minsky, *Any Woman's Blues: A Novel of Obsession* by Erica Jong, 2000. 10 x 7 x 3 inches (25.4 x 17.8 x 7.6 cm). Wood and wood veneers, inset leather panel; a binding in the style of a writing box; opening the box shows a tray containing writing paper and a fountain pen, when closed, the tray reveals a rattan lining that is also the book's endpaper. From the collection of Erica Jong. *Photo by the artist.*

Richard Minsky, *Sappho's Leap,* by Erica Jong, 2003. 7 x 12 inches (17.8 x 30.5 cm). Papyrus endpaper, inkjet printed with reproduction of Sappho text; wood end caps with oil-base stain, 23K gold leaf, polyurethane and lacquer, brass bushing; scroll cover is lacquered inkjet adapted from Greek Krater image of Alcaeus and Sappho bound as scroll. From the collection of Erica Jong. *Photo by the artist.*

Robert Warner, *Emily Dickinson, Fame,* 1998, 2003. 6 x 4½ x 3 inches (15.2 x 11.4 x 7.6 cm). Mixed media collage; letterpress printed; box binding.

Photo by Louise Millmann.

BARBARA MAURIELLO

Dolph Smith

Whimsical. Imaginative. Sculptural. Dolph
Smith's books engage the reader in narratives
that both delight and enlighten. On first
viewing, his work seems a total departure
from the traditional characteristics of the
book. On second glance, his faithful
adherence to maintaining the anatomy of
the book—book block, binding, and
cover—is clearly seen.

Tennarkippi's Unfinished Bridge Attempting To Cross The Rapids Of Jessie, 1994 to present. 20 x 27 x 5 inches (50.8 x 68.6 x 12.7 cm). Wood, copper, handmade paper, graphite, acrylic. Collection of Jessie Smith. *Photo by Steve Mann.*

Working At The Reach of My Headlights

Tennarkippi's Unfinished Bridge Attempting To Cross The Rapids Of Jessie, 1994 to present. 20 x 27 x 5 inches (50.8 x 68.6 x 12.7 cm). Wood, copper, handmade paper, graphite, acrylic. Collection of Jessie Smith. *Photo by Steve Mann.*

I am trying to imagine what it would be like to encounter a book for the first time. It may have been a first toy or a first tool, but that was a long time ago. The earliest book I remember was one printed on cloth. It was soft and wrinkled like my Grandmother's cheek. I liked rubbing it against my own cheek and I think I even slept with it. Being so flexible, it must have fit comfortably in my lap. I wonder today what it must have smelled like new, and what I would have heard when I turned a page. A

whisper? A rustle? I don't think it's too curious that as I begin to write down my feelings about the books I make that I recall an object that I reacted to with all of my senses. Surely that guides me to this day.

My initial instinct in beginning a book is to decide how I lift my work toward the reader. How do I, whether seriously or playfully, present them with a more animated apparatus asking to be held, moved, felt, heard, really interacted with? There are books one curls up with and there are books we go one-on-one

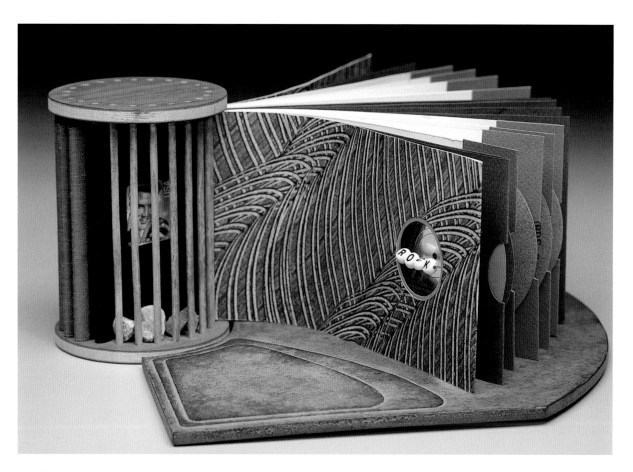

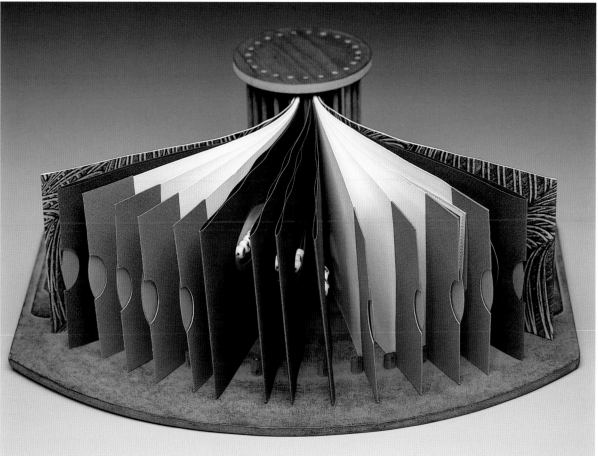

Rock And Roll, 2002. 5 x 13 x 10 inches (12.7 x 33 x 25.4 cm). Wood, paper, rocks, marbles, commemorative stamps, letter beads; the book sections are sewn onto the bars of the jailhouse spine; Elvis hits are all through the book on round pages that spin and spell out the lyrics. *Photo by Steve Mann.*

with. Light reading, heavy reading. I make the latter. My books, you lift, handle, weigh. Something implores me to take the book, as toy or tool, beyond the pedestrian function. I love to quote the great sculptor, Isamu Noguchi. In his book *A Sculptor's World*, he writes, "There is a difference between actual cubic feet of space and the additional space that the imagination supplies. One is measure, the other an aware-ness of the void—of our existence in this passing world." Does that explain why I make the books I make? No, but it's a beginning, because I can tell you that Noguchi's notion informs my work. My books are weighted toward the narrative. The story will come first.

I am not making books to be especially beautiful. Beauty is a grand aspiration but, for me, the beast—con-

Third Wonder: Ten-narkippi's House Of Seven Fables, 1995. 25 x 27 x 7 inches (63.5 x 68.6 x 17.8 cm) Mixed wood, acrylic, cord. This is a seven volume set; each book is removable, with moving parts, sounds, and hinged roofs that raise to reveal illustrations. Collection of Michael and Tempe Thompson.
Photo by Steve Mann.

DOLPH SMITH

tent—must be heard, even at the expense of craft. If I feel like my hands lack a particular skill, I try not to let that get in the way of the story. Unrefined edges bring with them the honest evidence of the hands. Some of my best pals have the informal presence of those who are true to themselves and, as a result, I find them more approachable and more interesting. As painter Hope Chafetz, the central figure in John Updike's novel *Seek My Face*, maintains, "Her susceptibility to beauty, Hope has always known, is what has kept her minor as an artist. The great ones go beyond beauty ... "

Now I would like to add another thought that is part of making these books, and therefore part of explaining why I make them the way I do. This one concerns "acts of nature." To begin, I have to admit something: I'm a fraud. I come from a painter's background. A watercolorist, if I hold to the full truth. A watercolorist, then a papermaker, then a bookmaker—who's also a sculptor. But that's getting ahead of my story, which is that I did not make my first good watercolor until I had discovered the one and true perfect attribute of that medium: that watercolor is an act of nature. Yes, no matter what one does with a brush onto the paper or "wet in wet"—applying pigment to wet paper—what happens during the next few moments is an act of nature of inescapable proportions.

During the wet and charged life of the watercolor wash, pigments move about, blend, settle erratically, and stain. Some pigments, as they interact with each other, create passages impossible to make with a brush; one color gives way to another. The grittier pigments settle as bold textures into the interstices of the paper and—most wonderful of all—because a watercolor does not dry evenly, the edgy, crisp watermarks are created. One of my favorite colors, Davy's Gray, in an effort to return to its origins, actually separates into the three colors from which it was blended. All of these small acts of nature are what give the watercolor life. As Noguchi would see it, this is a perfect collaboration between the artist's measure and nature's void. The notion of always being on the lookout for acts of nature has now become ingrained in my thought process. Although I don't know that I'm always successful in capturing acts of nature in my books, I simply cannot work without that aim in mind.

One more rambling thought and then maybe I can get around to making some sense, and helping you make sense of the books I make: I practice fidelity to the classic characteristics of the book. I want to be absolutely

From *Third Wonder: Tennarkippi's House Of Seven Fables.* Left to right: Sounds, House Boat, Bridge Between the Windows. *Photo by Steve Mann.*

Roll Your Own: A Journal Of Random Thoughts, 1995. 3½ x 4 x 6 inches (8.9 x 10.2 x 15.2 cm). Wood, leather, shredded text, and rubber bands. This is a self-printing book, read by filling the book block cage with the shredded text, winding up the "binding," or drive shaft, and placing it on the floor; the book will then roll forth and print the text. *Photo by Steve Mann.*

certain from the beginning that I have a clear feel for the book's anatomy. This comes from many years in the classroom teaching life drawing. Early devotion to drawing fundamentals is the necessary foundation on which all expressive drawing is based. To illustrate this, let me share an experience related by a dear friend of mine, a

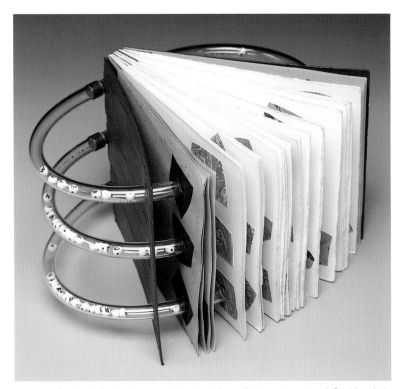

Book With Running Water, 2001. 6 x 8 x 10 inches (15.2 x 20.3 x 25.4 cm). Graphite, vinyl tubes, letter beads, marbled paper. The vinyl tubes on which the book is bound create the traditional three haiku lines. The tubes run inside the book, therefore carrying the haiku/water into the book. From a series of movable-type books. *Photo by Steve Mann.*

painter, about her first drawing class. The professor had set up a number of objects and the students were to draw them in direct line only. My friend became quickly bored and, determined to impress her teacher, began to add shading. After a while the teacher pulled a bench up next to hers and very gently said, "I see you are interested in shadow. That's good. But when you add shading to poorly drawn forms you don't have a better drawing, you just have a poor drawing with shading." I can never forget that story because a few years later that same professor pulled a bench up beside me and offered similar advice.

The anatomy of a book, as I see it:

1. *The book block.* That part of the book generally meant to gather, hold, and present the content.

2. *The binding.* Engineering meant to hold the book block securely together and at the same time allow the reader access to the content. The binding may also direct the reader along a particular path, or on several paths.

3. *The case or boards.* Traditionally the boards serve two functions: to contain and protect the book block and binding, and to invite the viewer/reader to engage the book visually, actively, or both.

Each of my books is anatomically correct, so to speak. If I see my books as having anatomy and not parts, it is infinitely more enabling in my search for that act of nature I am so needful of. As self-evident as this notion seems, I never begin a piece of work without pulling the thought into full view of the mind's eye. This can keep me from being tempted to shade a poor drawing. So now, with these thoughts about the narrative, acts of nature and anatomy in mind, how to get started? The phobia for "fear of getting started" should have a name! I would insert it here as the first challenge to face and overcome.

I use a lot of wood in building my sculptural books. A book may begin with a visit to a lumberyard specializing in fine woods. There will be a selection of shorts, boards with knothole flaws, basswood blanks for carving duck decoys, and always cutoffs planed to a surface that I can glue up successfully with the limited set of clamps I have. Impulse buying rules; there's no rush to see a book among the wood I am pitching into the cart. Back in the studio, I begin a series of tasks in search of an idea. I may begin a kind of childlike play with the blocks, looking for a match suggesting two covers of a book. Pairing,

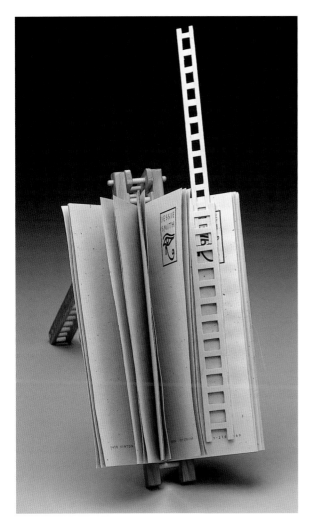

Ladder Back, 1997. 13 x 8 x 26 inches (33 x 20.3 x 66 cm). Wood, old stationery; sewn traditionally onto extension ladder. *Photo by Steve Mann.*

stacking, doodling in a sketchbook, I look for the sculptural sense. I look for a pairing of blanks that seem to be seeking a connection—a subtle invitation into a developing aura. If after a few days nothing has happened and I am collapsing in despair, I will just take a couple of wood blocks and cut part of them away with my band saw. That hurts, but it brings discord, which animates the space. Create a rough edge. Move from the formal to the informal. You see, I am trying to find narrative before I find a book. Wash my mouth out with tung oil, but I believe in story before craft. If I find the story, I can make the book. If I make the connection I enter Noguchi's "additional space."

At the same time that I'm pushing the blocks around and cutting into them, I'm usually roughing out some thumbnails in my sketchbook. They're the gesture drawings of my activity of looking for a relationship between the sculptural forms (the case) and the book block. These are the two dominant forms and their relationship

is crucial—I'm looking for the binding that brings them together. I like to think that at this stage I'm challenging another old cliché, "form follows function." Instead I cause function to follow form!

But, a word of caution about overdrawing. When I was doing so many watercolors, I never did much preliminary drawing. I worried about two things: that too much drawing would begin to bleed away the spontaneous energy inherent in the medium, and that watercolor—having a mind of its own—never conformed to the dang drawing anyhow! Winslow Homer comes to mind. He would start with a couple of rough lines to break up the space and just as likely ignore them. Instead, as soon as I sense my flat doodling has gone from aimless meandering toward something more concrete, I put the sketchbook away and begin to pick up the materials and tools. I can't always anticipate 3-D solutions in a 2-D format. I would rather make mistakes in "real scale"—react to things my hands are feeling rather than drawing. Throughout the many steps required in my books, I have long realized the value of taking the time to work out problems by building small models. It may take an hour or so to rough out an idea with scrap pieces, but I will have solved a problem and can then approach the final

Bridge of the Great Visible Binding: Historical Excavation In Eastern Tennarkippi, 1993. 22 x 30 x 3½ inches (55.9 x 76.2 x 8.9 cm). Wood, handmade paper, copper. Collection of Daniel J. Essig.

Photos by Steve Mann.

resolution with greater confidence and, this is very important, maintain the spontaneity.

In my book *The Great Visible Binding* the getting started came rather easily. While searching for an idea, I remembered the old saw about "water under the bridge." (You may have noticed I have a weakness for clichés. Maybe I believe in them because they have been around so long they have become a sort of comfort food for the mind.) I set up a pair of basswood blanks, established a distance between them, and then began the design of a bridge under which the water would pass. The bridge would be the spine of the book, and I felt if I could have the reader feel the pages flowing underneath as water they would relate that to the narrative flow of a good novel.

I now found myself at the point where I could employ my notion of collaborating with nature—an important part of my bookmaking philosophy. It was time to make the paper. True handmade paper can only be prepared in a beater, a machine that hydrates and fib-

rillates cellulose fiber. At this stage, the papermaker is able to direct the circumstances contributing to the qualities in the final paper, which includes translucency, rattle, tear strength, the way pulp takes color, and a variety of bonding situations. My experience over the years with making paper led me to choose an abaca half-stuff, a manila hemp fiber with high shrinkage factor that I like. I attempted to control the beating of the pulp so that there would be enough "acts of nature" in the final dried sheet to express the feeling of water. An extended beating time would give the resulting paper a crisp rattle leading to a rushing sound when the pages were leafed through.

I wanted long narrow sheets of paper to represent the flow of the water. The largest papermaker's mold I had was 18 x 24 inches (45.7 x 61 cm) so, using a sheet of ¾-inch (1.9 cm) builder's insulation blue board for my deckle, I cut five 2 x 21-inch (5 x 47.6 cm) openings. The deckle was then fitted to the mold face, enabling

DOLPH SMITH

me to make five long narrow sheets of paper at a time. This really expedited the papermaking, because the book had more than 150 sections totaling some 500 sheets of paper. Also, I knew that when the sheets were formed at the vat, a fair amount of pulp would slip under the deckle and in so doing create an exaggerated feathered deckle edge. Because of this, when the sheets were collated into sections and sewn, the edges of the book had the splashy organic look of a wave. Another controllable factor occurred during drying—only lightly restraining the paper as it dries encourages a rippling effect at the deckle. This is called edge wave. (How appropriate a name for an "act of nature.") In my mind's eye, I felt that combining all these properties together in the paper would lend themselves to the paper expressing the character of water. Natural colored pulp was used for a majority of the sheets. Some of the pulp was saved back and, using aqua-dispersed pigments, made into a variety of shades for the center sections. As for the sewing, I

used a very traditional method called sewing on raised cords, but I used wooden dowels to sew on so that I could build the book block into the bridge spine. In collating the sections, I sewed all plain sheets until I reached what I deemed to be the center of the book. Then I intermixed various blue sheets to emphasize the center of the stream, a highlighted moment in the progression of the narrative.

The book was finally done. Or so I thought. The book was in place, cradled between the bridge supports. The "water" flowed under the bridge and all seemed well. But there was a little surprise, just out of sight. When I removed the book from the cradle and turned it over to place it atop the pylons to read, the pages fell into disarray. "Woe is me," I first thought. Then I realized what had happened. The book had taken on a new life. The water was now going over the bridge. The pages had become rolling and billowing waves. Some pages fell to the side as if splashing out of the banks. I realized that

Tennarkippi's Bridge of Perpetual Waves, 1993. 21½ x 25½ x 4 inches (54.6 x 64.8 x 10.2 cm). Wood, copper, handmade paper, pulp painting. Collection of Tom Lee and Sheri Fleck Rieth.
Photos by Steve Mann.

this is why we make stuff. This is the joy of discovery. We tend to believe that as we make our work we are "being creative." But the creative act is when we come to share with Noguchi the awareness of the void.

I remember a riveting moment one evening at Penland School. Slides were being shown and during the opening introduction I heard a near perfect little story. It was about traveling at night through a dark and unfamiliar forest. The road was winding and foreboding and the driver could only see to the end of the automobile's headlights. But, as the story goes, the driver went all the way through the forest that way. That story has become something of a mantra to me. I relish beginning a book and finding myself facing a journey into the unknown. I love working only at the reach of my headlights.

Hands On

Dolph's signature book creations incorporate working parts. Here he demonstrates making *Tennarkippi Tales: Journey To Canterbury, which draws from the traditions of Venetian and Treasure bindings.*

Tennarkippi Tales: Journey To Canterbury, 2003. 20 x 21½ x 3 inches (50.8 x 54.6 x 7.6 cm). Wood, milk paint, copper, leather, graphite.
Photo by Steve Mann.

Sculpture as Books

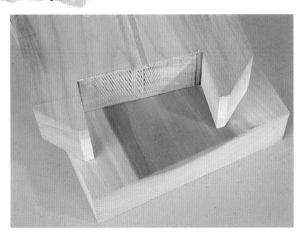

1. Two blocks of wood are selected and cut for the covers. The covers are the upright pieces shown in the photo above. This book will have a pair of ladders, so a table saw is used to create a groove in the outside of each cover to house the ladders.

2. I stack two identical strips of wood that are just the right height and width for each ladder and use a drill press to make holes for inserting the rungs. Using a miter box, the many pieces of dowel that are used for the rungs are hand sawn.

DOLPH SMITH

3. A small hammer taps one side of each rung into one side of the ladder.

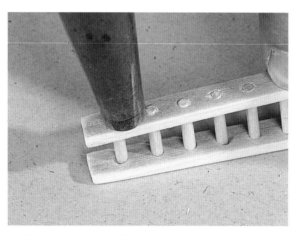

4. I have to work carefully as I tap the opposite side of the ladder into place since each rung must line up perfectly. A few taps secures everything in place.

5. After double-checking to see that each ladder will fit in the space created for it, a chisel is used to clean up the groove.

6. Now it's time to add surface decoration to each side of the covers. This is done by hand with a chisel and can take awhile.

7. After the chiseling work is done, a brush applies a coat of powdered graphite and shellac to the carved surfaces of the covers. (I also paint the ladders at this time.)

8. When the graphite mixture has dried, a soft cloth burnishes the surface of the covers and the ladders.

9. By carving and collaging, I can create a variety of textured surfaces that respond to the graphite high-lighting technique. These are samples of some finished pieces.

10. Here I'm hand-crinkling a sheet of 36-gauge copper foil. It cuts easily with scissors and is malleable enough to shape around eccentric forms.

11. A pair of needle-nose pliers turns under the sharp edges of the copper. This provides smooth edges and allows for neat overlaps when attaching a number of pieces to the cover blocks.

12. When it's time to attach the copper pieces, a tweezers holds each nail as I gently hammer it in place.

13. After the copper cladding is done, a solution of liver of sulphur is applied, which gives an immediate rich patina to the copper.

14. Burnishing the copper with a very fine steel wool makes it react the same way as the graphite—accentuating the wrinkled surface and creating bright highlights. In both techniques I stop once I've achieved the desired appearance.

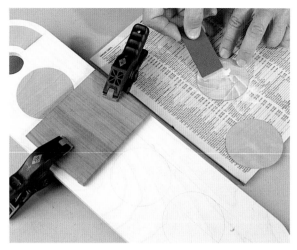

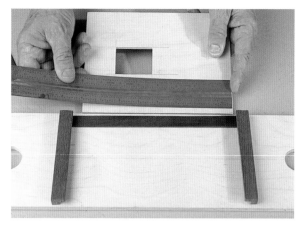

15. For the spine, a cabinet-grade piece of ⅜-inch (9.5 mm) birch plywood is cut to the right width and length to fill the opening in the center of each cover and to extend over each side for the spine. (Because a ladder will poke through each side overhang of the spine, I cut one hole in each of them.) Afterward, a series of circles and arches are cut from a sheet of air-craft grade 1/64-inch (.5 mm) plywood, and a design laid out for the top of the spine. A scrap piece of mat board applies glue to the backside of each wooden cut out. Once positioned, they are clamped securely until dry.

17. The spine is flipped over to determine how to hang the folios. Two pieces of wood for the hangers are attached, creating a track for inserting the folios. For sizing guides, I use a sample folio and the cloth binding I think I'll use for it.

16. After each piece has dried, I use a very fine grit sandpaper to gently round the edges of each image. Go easy with the sanding while watching for the layer of plywood to appear. This will be an indicator of how the finished milk-paint layers will look.

18. After flipping the spine over again, I brush on black milk paint—I'll go over the painted surface several times as it dries to stipple out air bubbles. After allowing this side to dry, the edges and opposite sides are painted.

19. After drying for two hours, the surface is gently wiped with #0000 steel wool to prepare it for the coat of blue milk paint.

20. Once the final coat of paint is dry, steel wool is used to work back through the layers of paint. I work the edges of the images just as I sanded them, waiting for the desired reveal of layers. This creates a shallow illusion of depth.

21. To prevent the folios from falling out of their hangers, a small hole is drilled in the spine at the end of each folio hanger and a small, movable stop is attached in each hole.

22. This book has four folios with each one telling a story. Because I want to have a window in each page of this folio, I cut slats for blinds and thread them together, make a windowpane and a window frame, and make the head of a woman who'll be in the window.

23. Sandpaper is used to texturize the surface of the lady, rounding the edges as I did with the circles and arches in step 16. Now it looks as if she's glowing.

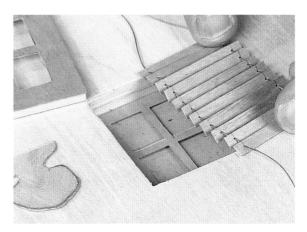

24. After attaching the outside windowpane, I place the wood blinds in the opening, trim the strings on the blinds, put the woman in the window, and secure the blinds and figure in place by attaching the inside windowpane. The blind has a double meaning: it represents one of the four main book structures, the Venetian bind, which is a book bound in two places.

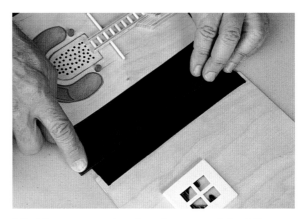

25. After constructing the other page of the folio, which features a window and a ladder, a hinged binding is created using book cloth.

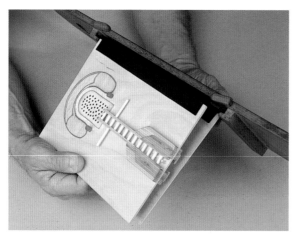

26. I slide the folio into place on the folio hanger. It fits!

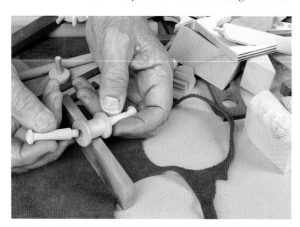

27. This phase of the book's design relates to the grand tradition of Treasure bindings, which feature carved and bejeweled covers. Instead I build toy-like miniatures to decorate the spine. Digging through my scrap parts—rounds of wood, bits of leather, and cloth—yields shapes and materials that can combine to make toys.

28. Another reason for making these objects is to address a theme at the center of my bookmaking. That is, I like to think of the book as a container of moving parts: 30 pages equals 30 moving parts. Therefore, my books all provide an interactive opportunity. Unlike pop-ups, these objects come out for use.

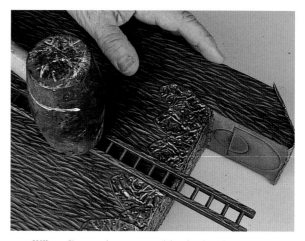

29. When I'm ready to assemble the book, I use a hammer to attach the ladder, which will come out, but I like it to be a tight fit. Below is side view of the finished book.

About the Artist

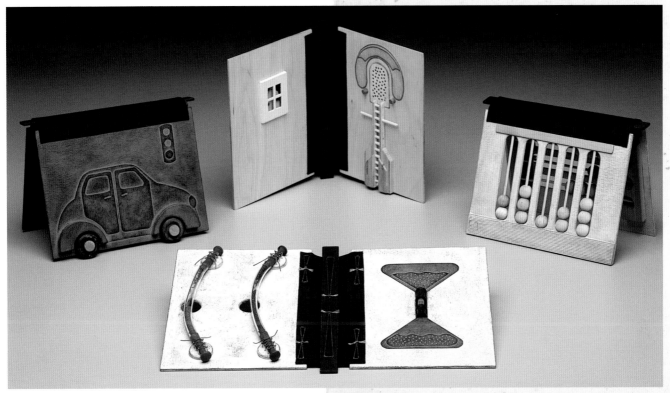

Above and below, folios from *Tennarkippi Tales: Journey To Canterbury, 2003.* 20 x 21½ x 3 inches (50.8 x 54.6 x 7.6 cm). Wood, milk paint, copper, leather, graphite. Photo by Steve Mann.

DOLPH SMITH works in his studio at Tennarkippi Field on Hurricane Hill in western Tennessee. He earned a B.F.A. from Memphis College of Art, Memphis, TN, where he also taught for 30 years, being elected Professor Emeritus in 1995. At the Memphis College of Art he founded The Flying Vat, a studio for teaching handmade paper and book arts. He has taught at Penland School of Crafts, where he co-taught sculptural book with Daniel Essig, and at Arrowmont School of Arts and Crafts.

He has received numerous awards, grants, and special distinctions throughout the course of his more than 40-year career. He is the recipient of the Art and Humanities Medal for lifetime achievement in Visual Arts and was the first individual recipient of the First Bravo Award from the First Tennessee Bank. He is a Charter Member of Friends of Dard Hunter, Society of Hand Papermakers.

His handmade paper, books, sculptures, and other artwork are collected around the world by private individuals, public and private corporations, colleges and universities, and museums. Individual collectors include former Vice President Al Gore, David Bowie, Seals and Croft, and the Cultural Minister of China. Dolph's artwork and writings have been featured in journals, magazines, and books, including *Surface Design Journal, The Complete Printmaker,* and *Hand Papermaking.*

Gallery

Hanging on a wall in my studio is this quote from Albert Einstein: "The laws of nature are so immutable that if it had not been for Newton, someone would have discovered the laws of gravity, but if Beethoven had not been born we would not have had the Eroika." As I prepare to write a statement about the artists represented in this gallery I am profoundly aware of what would have been missing from our lives if they had not been born.

Thanks Bill Drendel, for your wonderfully zany look at the world. Thanks Robbin, for making books that are still attached to your hands and heart. Thanks Bonnie, for your three-dimensional stories. Lynn, thanks for thoughts that have no beginning or end. That's as it should be if we are to live forever. And Dan? You know I'm going to embarrass you, don't you? There are two things I can never tell you: how much I respect you, and how much I love you. And finally, thank you to the one who's brought me the most joy and tears, my daughter, Allison. Thanks to all of you for being born.

Lynn Sures, *Water-Wheel Book*, 1998. 22 x 9½ x 9 inches (55.8 x 24.1 x 22.9 cm). Artist-made paper, cardboard, wood, metal, linen thread. *Photo by Chan Chao.*

William Drendel,
Gently, Oh So Gently
They Said No, 1998.
7¾ x 8¼ x 7¾ inches
(19.7 x 21 x 19.7 cm).
Japanese paper; altered book
emerging from gray cube.
Photos by the artist.

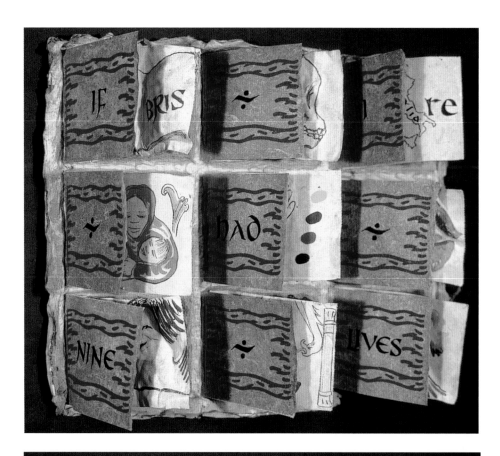

Lynn Sures, *If I Had Nine Lives*, 1999.
22 x 18 x 8 inches
(55.8 x 45.7 x 20.3 cm).
Cast paper pulp, wire,
acrylic, ink, linen
thread; screen print.
Photos by the artist.

Allison Smith, *Journal II: Cage*, 1996. 8 x 30 x 5 inches (20.3 x 76.2 x 12.7 cm). Steel, paper, wax. *Photos by the artist.*

Bonnie Stahlecker, *Bone Vessel*, 2002. 3⅛ x 2¼ inches (7.7 x 5.7 cm). Rib bones for covers, found text; sewn long stitch on manuscript. *Photo by the artist.*

Allison Smith,
*Journal I: Story of
Perception*, 1995.
16 x 16 x 8 inches
(40.6 x 40.6 x 20.3 cm).
Steel, paper, wax.
Photo by artist.

Robbin Ami Silverberg, *Snowstorm of Documents*, 2002. 10 x 15 x 6¼ inches (25.4 x 38.1 x 15.8 cm). Human hair, nails, hand stamping, Dobbin Mill papers; computer generated imagery and text. *Photo by the artist.*

Daniel Essig, *Golden Rectangles*, 2000.
5 x 4 x 4 (12.5 x 10 x 10). Handmade flax
paper, milk paint, tin, mica, ammonite
fossils; carved and painted mahogany.
Photo by Walker Montgomery.

Allison Smith,
*Journal III: Black and
White*, 1995.
18 x 17 x 10 inches
(45.7 x 43.2 x 25.4 cm).
Wood, paper, wax.
Photo by the artist.

Billy Riley, *Nativity Scene*, 1994. 14 x 12 x 20 inches closed (35.6 x 30.5 x 50.8 cm), 60 inches open (152.4 cm). Handmade paper, wood, leather, acrylic, glass. Collection of Dolph Smith. *Photos by Steve Mann.*

William Drendel,
Summer Reading, 1991.
10 x 10 x 10 inches
(25.4 x 25.4 x 25.4 cm).
Altered book bound with
blue nylon belt.
Photo by the artist.

Robbin Ami Silverberg,
Spun Into Gold, 2001-2002.
14 x 6 x 11¾ inches
(35.6 x 15.2 x 30 cm).
Computer generated text
on handmade Kozo paper,
bound and then cut and
spun into threads.
Photo by artist.

Jim Croft

*J*im Croft's love of wooden covers combine
perfectly with his skill as a woodworker.
Living a life of general self-sufficiency,
Jim is able to grow, make, or salvage the
materials he uses in his books. Dedicated
to recreating the old ways, he makes the
Gothic book. Though its roots are firmly
in the Middle Ages, Jim provides
contemporary book artists with a
technique that transcends time.

From Tree to Book

I was a somewhat disenchanted young man when I dis-
embarked my ship in Barcelona in 1970 after leaving
my on-board pantry-boy job. My desire to see the
world led me to Europe where I was surrounded and
magically infected by permanence and durability, what I
call a tried-and-true quality. I was immediately drawn to
the old—the way people lived centuries ago and how
they made the items they needed for everyday living.
The more I saw, the more I became interested in looking
at things that have lasted over the centuries. It all peaked
for me when I saw the Lindesfarne Gospel at the British
Museum. I ended up visiting it every day for a month. It
ignited my just plain love of the book.

Within a year I was branded with an uncompromising
passion for the pursuit of recreating the great books of
the wooden-board era. If you've seen a book from 1500
AD or earlier that's still in good shape, you understand.
This was the golden age of good materials and structure
being put to the test by a typically thick, heavy binding—a book with lots of support that still opens well.
Called the Gothic style, the books are made by the
drawn-on-boards method, where the closed covers lever-
age the spine, and clasps are incorporated as standard
book furniture.

In 1921, the great Dard Hunter displayed "the book
harmonious" at the Smithsonian. It was a whole book

"made by the hand of one man," recreating the old paper, type, and printing. Independently, I came up with a similar vision. I live a life of general self-sufficiency, which couples nicely with building books from the ground up. I'm able to provide all the elements of the book from what I grow, find in nature, or salvage. I grow flax and hemp and process them into thread and cord, make paper from old linen fire hoses, make parchment and leather, salvage wood from the tree to become the bookcover, and finally make the clasps from recycled brass and bronze.

The paper of the wooden-board era was made from fiber pounded to a pulp with a water-powered stamp mill. In 1990, Jack Thompson and I built such a mill below my pond. (Jack and I have co-taught *The Technology of the Medieval Book*, a hands-on workshop held at my place, for 10 years.) This further authenticated the paper I use since it comes from pre-1700 technology. I've been fortunate to have a loving partner, my wife Melody, who shares my self-sufficient tendencies. Using a spinning wheel, she makes strong and beautiful thread from raw flax fiber.

My technique is primarily about materials and structure. If you've been curious about wooden bookcovers, I hope this short chapter will help your understanding of using wood for books. Because wooden bookcovers aren't locked into place by fasteners or glue, which allows them to move more freely, they need to be made in a more precise way than other wood constructions. Even though I will be focusing on using hand tools for what I call, "the tree to the book," those who buy their lumber or are machine woodworkers should also benefit.

I like to remind my students that the origin of the word for book as an object is closely connected to the tree. If you look in the dictionary and trace the word "book," it comes from the word for beech in many languages. The Germanic root of book is *bok*, which also is the word for beech tree. In Old English, *boc*, is also a beech. Beech has a smooth bark and is easy to carve. The evolution of the book most likely progressed from carving figures or letters into the tree itself for the purpose of communication, to making tablets of beech that were carved into, to wood covers made of beech that protected a text block.

As I've traveled the country, I'm amazed by the amount of prime wooden bookcover material that is wasted by nature and "progress." Including pieces of firewood, there are greatly under-utilized resources of wood to salvage. A proper description of the best lumber for bookcovers would be air-dried, quarter-sawn, vertical-grain from a straight-grained tree also cut with the grain. Wood with these attributes, well known in the old days, is nearly impossible to purchase today.

In splitting wood one both reads the grain and eliminates unwanted areas. In general, quartering is the natural way that wood cracks on its own. When the wood is split or quarter-sawn (following the straight grain) it provides the most stable and strongest use of the material. The very center of the tree is the most unstable. The ultimate quartered wood has the longest medullary rays, which are made up of the wood grain that allows a tree to breathe from the heart to the outside. This grain runs perpendicular to what we usually consider grain. Oak is famous for having large medullary rays. The Italians call them mirrors; the English, silvery grain. The medullary rays are very subtle in many woods but can clearly be seen with slight magnification or by raking a light across the surface. Nature provides an easy guide to finding

Untitled selection of books, 1991 to present. 2 x 2 x 2 to 4 x 5 x 2 inches (5 x 5 x 5 to 10.2 x 12.7 x 5 cm). Handmade paper, commercial paper, brass, leather, woods: apple, yew, larch, Oregon maple, Oregon oak; pack-sewn double cords, leather spine; colored ink foredges in the experimental stage. *Photo by Ralph Bartholdt.*

these rays since wood generally cracks parallel to the rays as one cleaves the wood.

The hewing hatchet, or carpenter's side axe, was commonly found in a carpenter's toolbox before World War II. It can quickly prepare splits for the band saw or jointer, or in the case of nice-splitting wood, it can flatten one side of a thick stave so the machine planer can do the rest. This first step of rough flattening with the ax is a long lost link to working with quality materials. You could say working this way was a casualty of the industrial age. Once you flatten a side with an ax so it won't rock on a flat surface, you cross a significant historic barrier that takes you back to the old ways.

I first flatten the inside of the cover, that which faces the text. I leave extra length and thickness so I can easily detect any warp. Then I let it cure. High tannin woods such as oak and walnut will be harmful to paper if not fully cured. Wood historically used for preparing and holding food such as birch, beech, maple, or sycamore are more paper-friendly and require less curing time. If in doubt, I insert a temporary thin paper barrier between

the cover and text block and exchange the covers if the temporary paper becomes stained.

Curing wood is an art because there is so much variation in the nature of wood, even within the same tree. To oversimplify: beware of sudden changes. Green wood needs good air circulation and moderate dryness to cure. It will crack if dried too fast (though a little cracking on the ends is OK) or will mold if dried too slowly. Wood will always swell and shrink when exposed to different humidity, but a good piece of cured wood will remain flat once it's gotten used to its surroundings.

When clasped, even a large book will keep its shape no matter the humidity. This was important in the old days when books were rare and carried from place to place. It was necessary to have covers that could withstand traveling as well as extreme changes in climate, making the drawn-on-boards method ideal because it pulls the spine round, and squeezes air out. Because of this, it's very important to shape the inside of the board at the hinge to match the shaped shoulder of the text block. After I do this, I take down the outside of the covers near the hinge to make a smooth transition from spine to board.

Clasps make a special book even more special while protecting and preserving the binding and what's inside. Clasps were standard during the wooden-board era, but they are seldom made today, even for extremely valuable old books that once had clasps. Some of the reasons for this are the use of book boxes for conservation, the stability of today's climate control, and just the extra time, tools, and non-bookmaking skills involved in making clasps. There are many styles of clasps and I've chosen to illustrate one of the more common types in my Hands On section. It has a riveted brass hinge plate and catch plates, leather hinges, and a curved metal hasp.

When considering materials for a clasp, be sure to try a magnet on them. You want to avoid plated brass or bronze. Not only is the steel in it not as malleable as other materials, the corrosion from steel is quite damaging. Oddly a lot of old books were compromised in the moment of achievement, and are missing clasps because they had been attached with iron nails, and all that's left is black, rotten holes.

I find most of my brass and bronze at recyclers or at used building suppliers. It's cheap, it's old (to me that means more dependable), and tarnish is no prob-

Untitled, two-tone wood, 1998 to present. 4 x 6 x 2 (10.2 x 15.2 x 5 cm). Handmade paper, bronze, leather; Oak with tapered, dove-tailed splines of darker yew wood; construction is the same as used in historic antiphonals, no glue is used. *Photo by Ralph Bartholdt.*

lem. I use materials that are a dime's thickness and less. With old brass, I find I can bend it 360° without it breaking, pound sheet stock thinner, and make catch pins. Now that's malleable! However, modeler's shops should have some good new sheet for hinges and rod for rivets.

For working with wood and brass, I strongly suggest owning a farrier's rasp, a medium file, mill bastard, and smooth duct file. The farrier's rasp, used for shoeing horses, also beautifully shapes and flattens the edges on binder's board. When filing, file with the teeth pointed away from the tang (where the handle is) and with the file biting into the material. I often scold my students to "clean your files often if you want to get much done." When cleaning them, it's important to brush across the grooves between the teeth.

Clasps can hinge from either the top or bottom cover, making it a matter of personal choice. The ancients rarely recessed rivets and clasps into the cover since it was a lot of extra work, but I think it makes for a beautiful finish, not to mention being more neighborly to other books when shelved. You may notice my hasps curve in to match the curve of the fore-edge. This not only makes them easier to fit when you are attaching them, the curve of the hasp can be adjusted to tighten or loosen the fit of the cover to the text block as the environment (mostly meaning the humidity) thickens or thins the book. This is my invention, one of those serendipitous happy errors, developed after I made the hasp too long.

Untitled selection featuring hinge plates, 1998 to present. 3 x 4 x 2 to 5 x 7 x 2 (7.6 x 10.2 x 5 to 12 x 17.8 x 5 cm). Alum-tawed deerskin, leather, brass, bronze, woods: Oregon white oak, yew, California oak; pack-sewn double cords, leather spine. *Photo by Ralph Bartholdt.*

Hands On

Jim demonstrates how to make the Gothic book. He begins his "tree to book" by first selecting the right wood. The cover takes shape under Jim's hands from hand-hewing to drilling. He shows the fine rendering of the brass clasp from making a clasp pin to polishing the finished hinge plate.

Wood Covers and Metal Clasps

1. Good wood is everywhere, and few know where to find it. Top to bottom: Oregon white oak; California live oak; New Jersey Mulberry; Oregon big-leaf maple.

2. Splitting tools, including mallets hewn from small stumps and roots, splitting mauls and wooden wedges, short and large froes. It's important to take care of your tools. The curling of the ends in the metal wedges need to be ground or they can be dangerous.

3. An example of a nice split made from ash. Most woods split more evenly when halved rather than splitting small pieces from a large block.

4. I call this "fool the master." This wood looks like it has a perfect straight grain on all four sides, but once quartered, it reveals that it comes from a tree with an extreme left twist.

5. Once the boards are split and sawn, a pencil sketches in the guidelines that mark the prime spots for covers.

6. Following the adage, "Hew to the line, and let the chips fall where they may," the board is hand-hewn. The hewing hatchet or carpenter's side axe is still a useful tool for quick stock removal and rough flattening because its blade is flat on one side.

7. Finding any twists and high spots on the hewn board is done with the help of sight sticks. Using sight sticks is good for training the eye.

8. These are bundles of bandsawn wood tied, stacked, and stickered. The bundles are weighted as they dry, and the cords around the bundles allow for tightening as the wood shrinks.

9. A saw trims the edges of the boards, which have been placed on a large round of wood as a support with a 2 x 4 as a stop. Most people saw too hard. A good saw should be used with a nice relaxed motion. Nothing should wiggle.

10. There are many ways to hold a bookcover for planing. Since the plane cuts better at an angle, I've placed thin strips of wood between the jaws of the bench to hold the wood where it needs to be.

11. Planing the fore-edge and hinge edge is easy compared to planing the wide flat sides. You can clearly see the medullary rays on this California live oak.

12. This is an example of covers made totally by hand from tree to book. These are prime Oregon white oak book covers made from wood that was air-dried for 25 years.

13. Drilling the lacing holes for the cords at approximately 45° minimizes weakening of the board. Afterward, I'll cut a channel between the two drilled holes to allow the cords to be laid in.

14. A farrier's rasp shapes the edges. This rasp works especially well on the tricky end grain. Here you can see the cut channels mentioned in the last step.

15. These are examples of old salvaged brass and bronze. Included here are a door kick plate, door handle, anvils made from found metal, and bending and forming jigs made from scrap.

16. These rejected clasp parts show the different routes that I've taken in fabrication.

17. An awl scratches the outline of the pattern in the brass.

18. Tin snips quickly rough out the clasp shape. Any resulting distortions made by the snips are easily flattened after cutting. Using a jeweler's saw is another good way to arrive at the same result.

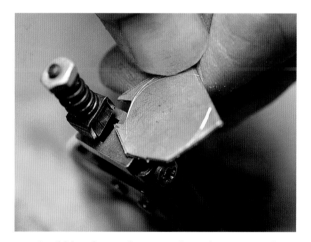

19. A nibbler shapes the piece. It easily removes the little rectangles left after cutting out the brass.

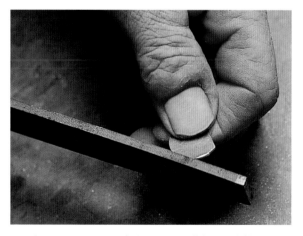

20. A common 10-inch (25 cm) mill bastard file is used to clean up the edges of the cut-out piece.

21. Using a drill as a lathe, a round jeweler's file incises the neck on the catch pin. Since this file can easily break, don't push too hard while working. In the background is a strip of parchment and piece of leather that are used for the hinges. Wrapping the leather around a core—in this case parchment, but it can be any other strong material such as Tyvek—makes it strong.

22. The "arrowhead" portion of the catch pin that will be driven into the cover is formed. Pounding stretches the pin while a nibbler shapes the head and trims the sides of the sharp point.

23. After shaping, the catch pin is ready to be driven in. The drill bit is the same diameter as the catch pin and is marked to the depth needed. The numbered drill gauge shown helps to coordinate these measurements. Notice the recess that has been cut in the other cover to receive the hinge plate.

24. A forming block modifies the heads of the brass escutcheon pins that will become the rivets.

25. A ball-peen hammer forms the head after placing the pin in the small hole. A hinge plate that has been drilled and is ready for riveting sits next to the block.

26. To drill the hinge plate, a center punch first made a dimple that now guides the drill bit.

27. End nippers leave the right amount of shank "standing proud" to form the rivet. For hammering the shank, a ball-peen hammer is used with the hammering alternating between the outside and inside of the bookcover. An anvil must always solidly support the rivet underneath when hammering.

28. A small coarse file takes down any excess left of the rivet. When the heads are nearly flush, the ball-peen hammer pounds the remaining head into the recess of the hinge plate.

29. A handmade hardwood punch and hammer set the hinge plate into the board.

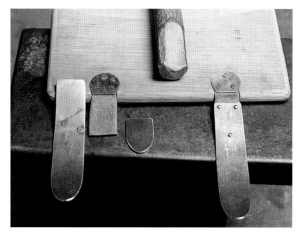

30. This shows the hasp (the long metal piece) with the back plate before riveting (left) and after riveting (right). The back plate is made from much thinner brass than the hasp. In order to determine the length of the hasp, I temporarily laced the wood covers for the text block, then removed them when it was time for riveting.

31. To accommodate the thickness of the leather, the hardwood punch is used to bend the back plate to meet the hasp.

32. A file brush, finishing file, a small coarse file, a fine riffler file, and a needle file are used in the process of finishing the rivets and hinge plates so they will look like one piece. All that's left to do on these hinges is to polish them with fine sandpaper and chrome polish.

33. This is thread Melody spun from raw flax fiber.

34. Pack-sewn or double-cords are appropriate for thicker, heavy books. Until the wooden covers could be applied, I protected the text block with temporary board covers.

35. The cover and text block are laced-in.

36. After lacing-in, the cover should spring open on its own. At this point, you can still shape the board as needed.

37. Softwood pegs with a long taper are made—working on the straight grain of the softwood avoids making any lumps in the pegs. After pasting the portion of the cords that will go in the holes and the pegs, a bone folder pushes the pegs in.

38. With the board supported, a ball-peen hammer makes the final taps on the peg.

39. End nippers cut the pegs and cords on the outside of the cover, then they're trimmed with a knife using a gentle sawing motion.

About the Artist

JIM CROFT has been making books for three decades, being a specialist in making books the "old-way." In 1987, Jim, along with Jack Thompson, began a two-week workshop at Jim's rural homestead in Idaho to teach *The Technology of the Medieval Book.* Book artists and enthusiasts who participate learn to build a book from the ground up, which includes making alum-tawed leather from goat skin or deer hides, fashioning and carving the covers, making parchment, and fabricating brass clasps. Jim is also renowned for his fine hand-crafted book-making tools. Jim gives workshops around the country on making the Gothic book and on toolmaking. He has taught at Penland School of Crafts and the Paper and Book Intensive.

Gallery

Thomas Eliot Conroy, *Blank Notebook.* 6¾ x 10 inches (17.1 x 25.4 cm). Black walnut boards, linseed oil finish, biscuit Harmatan goatskin spine; herringbone sewing; vellum spine liner and endpapers; tight back. *Photo by Steve Woodall.*

I've enjoyed book conservation, restoration, and repair over the years. I've worked on everything from circulating-library paperbacks to 500-year-old leather-covered wooden boards with brass clasps. I've taken classes from many accomplished book-arts practitioners. Yet, I see this current time as an exciting one for all imaginable forms of book art. The level of communication, sharing of skills, and talent of today's book artists are unbelievable. I see them incorporating historical lessons that take their work into the realm of art and crosses boundaries we didn't even know were there.

My gallery contains some of my personal hall-of-fame candidates for their original research and for being "worship-full," while still remaining humble in approach. Tom Conroy: nobody knows how much he knows about books because ten percent of his brain is unknowable. He has nicknamed me Book Bodger. Pamela Spitzmueller: Clark Kent-like, straight Harvard conservator by day, materials and structure researcher and practitioner by night and weekends.

Hedi Kyle: the Michael Jordan of book arts and conservation—a one woman think tank whose range of influence is difficult to fathom. I'd also like to acknowledge Jack Thompson, Dan Flannagan, and Gary Frost for their continued inspiration.

Thomas Eliot Conroy, *Teaching Genealogies of American Hand Bookbinders,* 1992. 5½ x 8½ inches (14 x 21.6 cm). Olive-green Harmatan goatskin, gold tooling, black goatskin onlays; pallets and gouges cut by the binder; herringbone sewing; vellum spine liner; tight back. *Photo by Georgianna Greenwood*

Pamela Spitzmueller, *Long and Link Stitch Sampler,* 1986. 10½ x 6½ x 2½ inches (26.7 x 16.5 x 6.4 cm). Paper, vellum, bone button, colored linen thread, alum-tawed skin; mother of pearl button; mechanical tightback binding (the sewing thread attaches textblock directly through the spine of wrapper); sampler of stitches on spine. *Photo by the artist.*

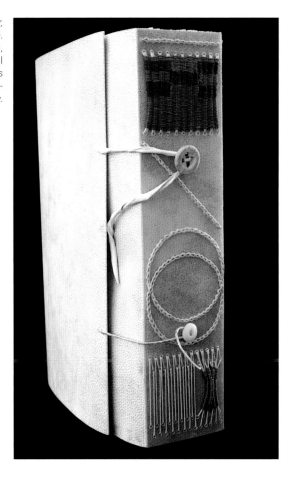

Pamela Spitzmueller, *Two Brothers,* 1988. 4 x 5 x 9 inches (10.2 x 12.7 x 22.9 cm). Wood, thread, parchment, paper, buttons; idealized models of medieval German traditional link-stitch bindings using rigid wooden spines. *Photo by the artist.*

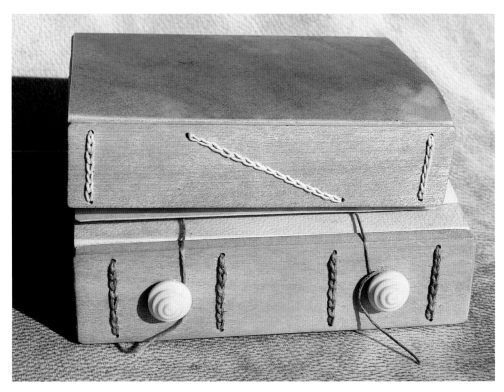

Hedi Kyle, *One Sheet Book with Folder,* 1999. 4 ¾ x 8 x ¼ inches (12 x 20.3 x .6 cm). Paper. *Photo by Paul Warchol.*

Hedi Kyle, *Square Pockets,* 1999. 6 x 6 x½ inches (15.2 x 15.2 x 1.3 cm). Paper. *Photo by Paul Warchol.*

Pamela Spitzmueller,
The Off-White Book, 1995.
4 x 6 x 3½ inches (10.2 x
15.2 x 8.9 cm). Handmade
paper, oak boards, wild
peccary skin, thread, bone
buttons. *Photo by the artist.*

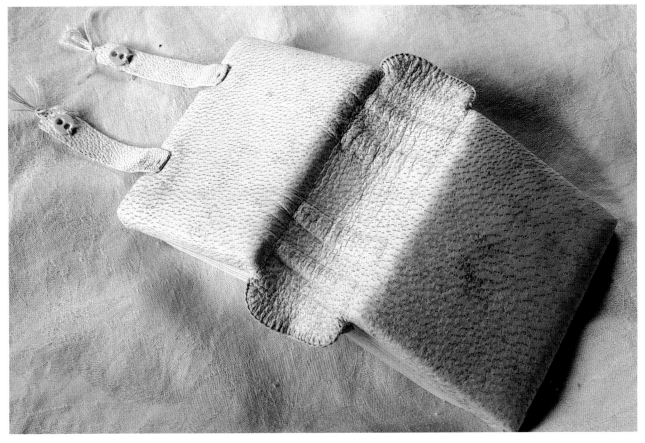

Julie Leonard

In creating altered books, Julie Leonard seeks to build relationships between memory, words, and meaning through the visual presentation of language. In order to fully invite the reader into her work and engage them in the narrative, Julie has developed structures that enable her to present book forms that read in a similar manner to the codex.

al pha bet, 1999. 4 x 10 inches (10 x 25 cm), closed. Wood and metal type, letterpress printed linoleum block; French-door link stitch binding. *Photo by David Trawick.*

Layering Meaning

Field Study—Elements of Botany, 2001. 5½ x 8½ inches (13.8x 21.3 cm). Cut book pages, mat board, varnish, graphite; collage.
Photo by David Trawick.

"The blank spaces of the night, the blinding whiteness of the page before print, offer themselves to the fantastic, to a reading of fire or the tracks of animals..."

—*Susan Stewart*

Books speak to me of age and the past. As a child, I lived in books, reading late into the night by flashlight under the covers, or with the crack of light from the hallway. I was drawn to the old ones. The object itself as much as the stories within fascinated me; the handwritten signatures, anonymous scribbles, the smell of the pages, the feel of the paper and of the type, the romance of the illustration, the shape of the words, the touch of old boards, gilding and cloth, the texture. I wanted to be absorbed by books, to enter an old world.

In *On Longing*, Susan Stewart describes nostalgia as a particular kind of longing, a yearning for that which not only does not exist in the present, but never existed and is thus unattainable. I was born nostalgic. For me, nostalgia and memory intertwine. It is in books that I find myself searching for that unattainable something. Books possess a collective aura, all books existing in one book, all stories in one story.

In my book work I try to reflect the blurring of lines at the intersection of memory and nostalgia. I build relationships that are not fixed or even necessarily clearly understandable, just as memory is not fixed. In doing so, I seek to evoke a mood or emotion, leaving room for the viewer/reader to bring his or her own sense of memory into the work. I want them to read the books like a poem for the sounds and shapes of the words—an object expressing meaning purely by its form.

I am fascinated with words and the ever-shifting nature of meaning in language. The book, with its

JULIE LEONARD

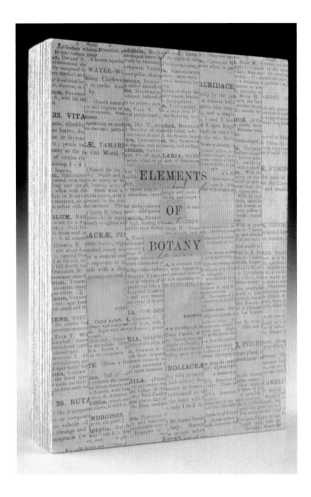

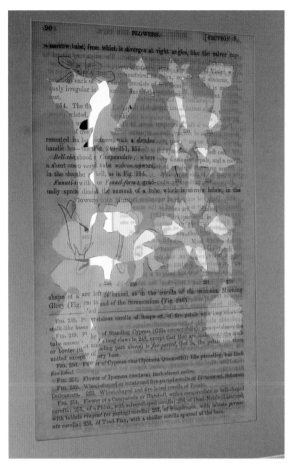

Front view and detail. *Field Study—Elements of Botany,* 2001. 5½ x 8½ inches (13.8 x 21.3 cm). Cut book pages, mat board, varnish, graphite; collage.

Photo by David Trawick.

intimate size and nature, is a perfect medium in which to explore memory and its relationship to storytelling and language. The serial nature of the book form allows me to create either an actual narrative or a sense of narrative. It provides a place to look at continually recurring themes—mystery and spirit, lineage, text and image, text as image, and craft.

For the last several years, my work has revolved around the visual presentation of language. Meaning is fluid, each word filled with the nuances of context, gesture, and inflection, which translates to another kind of nuance when language is presented visually as text. This includes the pictorial aspects of letterforms and text, and the implied meanings that can be derived from text even when it's partially or completely unreadable.

The word text has root origins in texture, textile, weaving. Content is necessarily selective. We create stories by inclusion and omission. Obscuring the text, changing the weave, can represent that selectivity. Using a nonlinear or partially unintelligible text, patched together from a range of sources, is a way to suggest that it possibly could be arranged or told in a different way. You can build a sense of secrecy or mystery, a layering of information.

In exploring this area, I began to work with altering existing texts. In looking at altered-book work, I was particularly drawn to artists who altered the actual pages rather than drawing into or over the pages—those who would rip, cut, or fold existing pages, rearranging the order and format of the structure. I first saw works by Scott McCarney and Buzz Spector that were worked in this manner. Then, at a show in St. Louis, I saw a piece called *Twisting Silence* by Linda Barron that had a quality I had never seen. The pages had been ripped, and lines and fragments of text had been cut out and reattached with the thread from the original sewing. The book had an incredible sense of age, of moving through time, and of absorbing all the experience, wear, joy, and grief of life. It resonated with that sense of reaching for a nonexistent past that lives in me. That piece in particular led me to experiment with altering existing texts.

The books I work with are old reference and

Fragments, 2001. 5 x 6 x 3 inches (12.5 x 15 x 7.5 cm), closed, 6 x 80 (15 x 200 cm), open. Found and handwritten text, cut pages, watercolor; collage, accordion-fold stiff leaf structure. *Photo by David Trawick.*

Shrouded Passage, 1999. 10 x 25 x 1 inches (25.4 x 63.5 x 2.5 cm). Torn book pages; decoupage, watercolor. *Photo by David Trawick.*

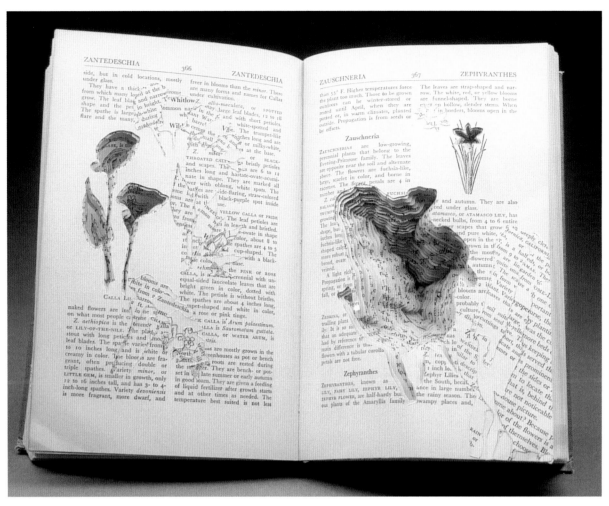

Layering Time, 2000. 6 x 9 inches (15 x 22.5 cm). Ink; cut book pages that move progressively into book, collage, drop-spine enclosure. *Photo by David Trawick.*

botany books—old because of the sense of a lost time and quality they evoke; reference books because of a love of words and their meanings, origins, and relationships; and botany books because they are beautiful and bring the natural world into a closed and intimate space. Bodies. Plants. Books. We describe each with the parts of the other. Head, tail, spine, roots, stem, arms, leaves, foot.

In beginning to experiment with this process, I left the book in its original binding. I would go into the book and rip or cut pages, creating patterns and depth, a kind of drawing. In this work, I would bring all the pieces of the original book back in. If I ripped out pages, I collaged or sewed them on to other pages or added them to a frame or enclosure that contained the book. While I was interested and pleased with these pieces, I found them difficult to read. As a series of pages became one image, leafing through the original book seemed awkward. While the pages worked as individual images, they lost the sense of narrative I was

looking for. I wanted another form of presentation.

While continuing to alter existing texts, I began removing the pages from their original bindings and reworked them into new binding structures that retained the serial nature of traditional book forms, allowing the reader to page through the book. Since book structure has always been a primary interest for me, putting these altered pages into my own bindings marked a return to this earlier interest.

When I first started bookbinding, I focused on learning solid bookbinding skills and understanding the underlying structure of book forms. I worked with a variety of structures, making blank books for use as albums, journals, guestbooks, etc. I wanted to produce pieces that were functional, structurally interesting, and aesthetically pleasing. In this work, I was already concerned with the role structure played in the quality, nature, and function of each book.

Artists use the book form as a means of expression for a variety of reasons. The codex has held a unique place in human consciousness since its inception. Early books were rare, valuable, and revered. This value lay both in the content, a mystery to most in a primarily non-literate society, and in its physical presence, as the writing and binding of a book was a time-consuming and painstaking process. Initially, most books were religious texts of some kind, which imbued them with an even greater sense of value. In some manner, the medieval concept of books as holy or magical remains with us today. Our collective association with books as carriers of knowledge and wisdom comes from a time when they were not a mass-produced item. Artists can make use of these cultural associations when working in book form. Text, image, and structure can all be used in building a piece that makes use of the history, associations, and craft of bookbinding to express its meaning.

Book artist and historian Johanna Drucker, in her *The Century of Artist's Books*, makes a distinction between books that provide "an experience associated with books themselves" and books that move into a more sculptural realm that "function as icons of bookness or book identity." I am concerned primarily with the former; books that function traditionally, but that challenge the viewer's expectations when reading or receiving information in that format.

While the structure of my books varies, I keep the sense of a traditional book by using narrative and including pages that turn, retaining the serial nature of the book. Artist's books that use traditional book

Julia, 1990. 10 x 8 x 1½ inches (25.4 x 20.3 x 3.8 cm). Handwritten text, photocopied images; accordion flag structure. *Photo by Tom Mills.*

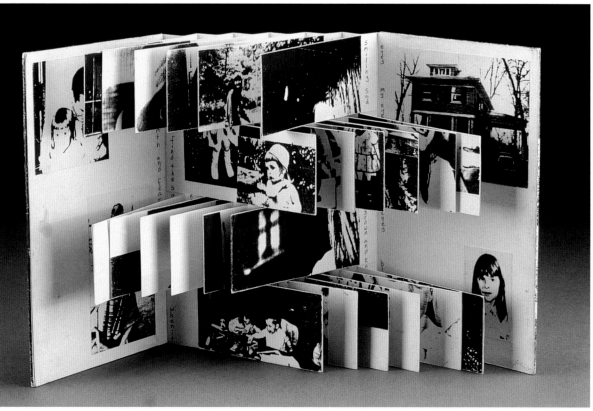

JULIE LEONARD

In Full Bloom, 2003. 4 x 4 x⅜ inches (10 x 10 x .9cm). Handmade flax paper with inclusions; letterpress printed, metal type, stiff leaf structure. *Photo by David Trawick.*

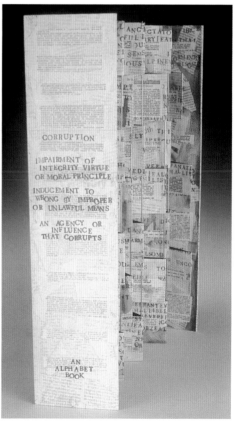

Corruption, 2003. 18 x 4 x 12 inches (45 x 10 x 30cm), closed. Steel rods, found text, gesso, collage, rubber stamp; accordion-fold structure. *Photo by David Trawick.*

forms require the reader to look and look again. To fully experience this kind of book, you must hold it, be close enough to see small text or images, participate by opening covers, turning pages, and reading. It requires time, a slowing down and settling in.

These types of artist's books, in contrast to sculptural book work, are difficult to exhibit. If treated as artistic objects and shown in conventional art forums such as galleries and museums, they are often put under glass and are untouchable. In this case, only one view of an interactive form is seen. This problem has been discussed extensively: How does one exhibit artist's books? Where do you display them? How can they be shown and seen effectively?

Solutions range from providing gloves and allowing them to be handled, to presenting only a single spread and keeping them under glass. However, even when a book can be handled, the environment of the gallery or museum does not lend itself to reading. Some artist's books take hours to read as any book does. You need a comfortable chair, a quiet room, and a lot of time. This is not how most viewers move through an art exhibit.

In struggling with how to display artist's books that are more traditional in form, I thought about what was successful about sculptural book work. How could some aspect of that be brought into books that have multiple views? In my own work I found one solution in making pieces that operate on several levels. Using structure, I build layers of meaning so that the piece successfully conveys ideas in varied environments.

For example, you can create a book that works on three successively complex levels. The first level works when the book is viewed as an object that cannot be touched or manipulated. A second level is added when the viewer is able to handle the piece. A final level is revealed when the viewer is able to fully engage with the piece by reading it. The artist can work with text/image relationships, experiment with writing styles, make passages through pages not continuous, and shift the content from text to image to structure and back.

An example of this is my book, *fifty-two words*. This book makes use of a stiff leaf structure that is described in the Hands-On section of this chapter. It is a small book with 52 pages made of boards, each page containing one word, a cut-out symbol for that word, a lightly printed phrase, and the word repeated across the entire surface as an overall texture. It is a long, stocky, chunky object. On first viewing, it

fifty-two words, 2001. 4 x 4 x 9 inches (10 x 10 22.5 cm), closed. Cut out pages, dyed papers; laser-printed text, stiff leaf binding structure, drop-spine enclosure. Edition of 10. *Photo by David Trawick.*

JULIE LEONARD

Various views. *fifty-two words*, 2001. 4 x 4 x 9 inches (10 x 10 x 22.5 cm), closed. Cut out pages, dyed papers; laser-printed text, stiff leaf binding structure, drop-spine enclosure. Edition of 10.
Photo by David Trawick.

creates an arc where only about one-third of the pages can be seen at once, providing a glimpse of pages where the text creates a visual texture.

When the reader is able to handle the book, it acts like a slinky, allowing you to flip through the pages as it moves. At this level, you see cutout shapes and each word printed in bold text. When paging through slowly, page by page, the lightly printed phrases referring to the word and shape on each page are revealed. My hope with this piece was that each viewing worked on its own, that there was a sense of resolution when the book could only be seen from one point, and that each further level enhanced its meaning.

Structure becomes an integral part of content. It helps to tell the story. As with my production work, I am still concerned with creating objects where structure builds on the function and meaning of the piece. I also want the work to be beautiful in some way. Recently, I found a book of essays entitled *Uncontrollable Beauty* that examines the nature and place of beauty in contemporary art and culture. In his essay, James Hillman says,

> We want the world because it is beautiful, its sounds and smells and textures, the sensate presence of the world as body. In short, below the ecological crisis lies the deeper crisis of love, that our love has left the world. That the world is loveless results directly from the repression of beauty, its beauty and our sensitivity to beauty. For love to return to the world, beauty must first return...Beauty cannot enter art unless the mind in the work is anchored beyond itself so that in some way the finished work reflects the sacred (the world) and the doing of the work, ritual.

This relationship of beauty and art to the natural world makes sense to me, as does the notion of ritual as a part of artmaking. We are a culture searching for soul. My house is full of icons. They are marks of love, of superstition, of faith, and of protection. In the attempt to find a place for the soul and spirit of life, I make books. This is where ritual enters, and repetition. The work of the craftsperson: forging a horseshoe one hundred times … throwing a thousand bowls on the potter's wheel … ripping and cutting pages over and over again … sewing and binding books … It is like meditation or prayer.

Hands On

Julie demonstrates basic stiff leaf structure and five variants that can be devised from it. These structures work well for artists' books because they function similarly to traditional codex or accordion-fold books. They provide a way to build up pages with varied materials and thicknesses. By using frames, windows, or insets, the structures make it possible to incorporate found text, images, and reworked pages into a newly constructed book. Julie thanks Scott McCarney and Pamela Spitzmueller for introducing her to the basic form of this structure.

Basic Stiff Leaf Structure

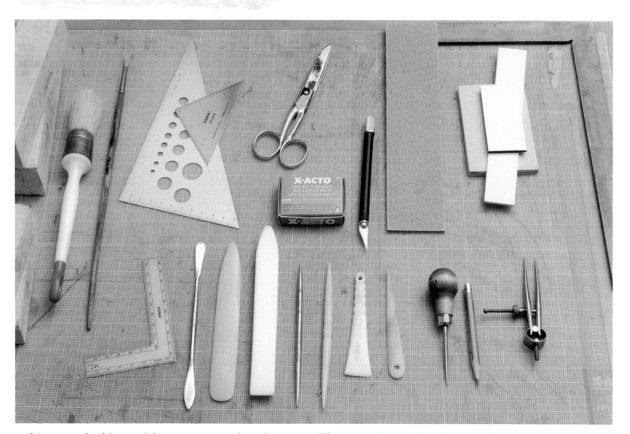

1. It's easy to build a model using paper and masking tape. This provides a guide when attaching pages, and lets you figure out ordering and binding methods beforehand. Shown are useful tools, jigs, and templates to use in this work.

JULIE LEONARD

2. Cut the pages to size. For this model I used four-ply museum board. If a board shear is not available, cut the pages using a metal square to ensure accuracy. All the pages, plus a few extras, are cut at once.

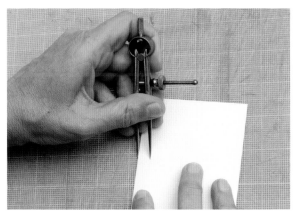

3. To determine hinge placement, one of the extra boards is marked along the spine edge. Hinge material will cross the joint area and extend onto each board. The finished look for the book determines how much of the hinge should extend on each board, but I always use a minimum of ½ inch (1.3 cm) for secure attachment.

4. After cutting the hinge width off the marked board, that board is used as a template for marking the hinge placement on the other boards on both sides.

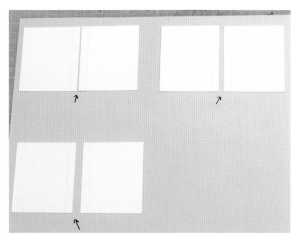

5. Here are examples of different joint widths. The joint, or space between the attached boards, allows the structure to expand. This space depends on the thickness of materials used on the pages.

6. I make joint jigs to varying thicknesses to accommodate attached materials. Since I am using fairly thin cloth hinges, the joint for this model will be one board thick.

7. The length of the hinge is about ¼ inch (.6 cm) taller than the boards, while its width is the joint width plus the amount the hinge will extend on each board.

8. For quick cutting of the hinge material, I use a template made of scrap board that is the width of the hinge and set a long strip of material up against a straightedge.

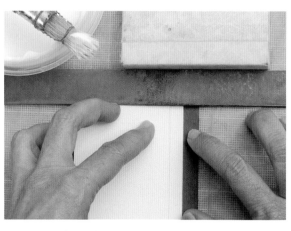

9. For attaching the boards to the hinge, the elements are aligned with a straightedge and PVA used to paste the area of the board to be attached to the hinge.

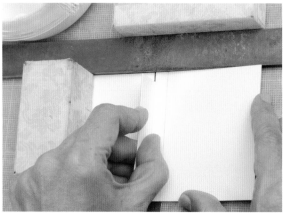

10. To adhere the boards to the hinge material, the joint jig is used to attach the second board correctly.

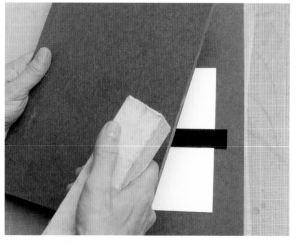

11. A joined pair is placed under weight to dry.

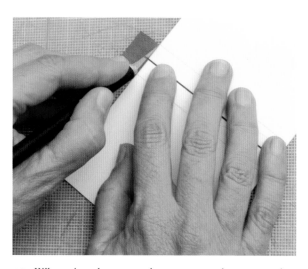

12. When dry, the excess hinge material is trimmed.

13. The pairs are folded with the hinge material on the inside.

JULIE LEONARD

14. Hinge the folded pairs in the same way as the individual boards.

15. I continue to hinge units of four pages, eight, etc., until all units are attached.

16. The completed text block

17. Here is a spine option. While the structure doesn't require a spine piece, it provides a more finished look. I attach the spine material to the front and back boards only. In order for the book to open well, I do not adhere the coth all the way to the board edge. Instead, I leave ³⁄₁₆ to ¼ inch (.5 to .6 cm) in from the board edge.

18. The finished model with the spine option.

Using the Image Material as the Hinge

One variant uses the image material as the hinge. The material needs to be strong enough to function as a hinge and support the weight of the board used as the substructure. When the image is acting as the hinge, the joint width can be quite narrow, approximately one-half of a board's width.

19. The full paper hinge is attached using a narrow joint. I find that cutting the paper oversize and trimming it out after adhering it to the boards is the easiest method.

20. Here are hinged pairs with board material. The pairs are attached as described in Basic Stiff Leaf Structure.

21. The finished model

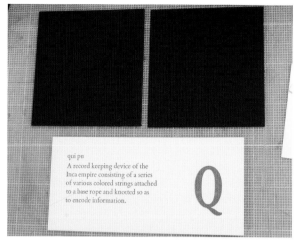

qui pu
A record keeping device of the Inca empire consisting of a series of various colored strings attached to a base rope and knotted so as to encode information.

Q

22. For framing the image area, the hinge material is made smaller than the boards.

23. Here, I'm attaching sets of four.

24. Here's the finished model with an optional cover made of separately covered boards that are then attached with PVA to the front and back of the boards of the text block.

Second Variant
Fully Covered Unit

In the previous examples, the edges of the boards remain uncovered. In certain situations, a fully covered unit is preferred. In order to do this, pairs of boards are covered and then fully attached. Thus each page is double thickness. The covering material (in this example book cloth is used) is cut to the size of two boards, plus the joint widths, plus ½ inch (1.3 cm) all around for the head, tail, and fore-edge turn ins.

27. After they dry under weight, the pairs are folded with the covered portion on the inside of the fold.

25. Adhere both boards to the cloth, using the joint jig to set the joint space while attaching the second board.

28. To relieve the tension in the fold at the head and tail, I make a small cut in the turn-in cloth at the joint.

26. The turn ins are made at the head, tail, and both fore-edges.

29. Using PVA, the pairs are attached as described in Basic Stiff Leaf Structure step 15.

THIRD VARIANT
Mats and Inserts

Creating a mat or inset allows images to be set below the surface of the page, which protects fragile materials and provides formality with the framing. For inset areas, cut pairs of boards, one solid and one with a window. Cut out, and adhere pairs together before covering. Extra care must be taken with the inset area. Before doing the turn ins, the cloth needs to be worked to fit into the inset. Cutting an X into the cloth at the inset allows the cloth to move and to be easily worked.

32. The book is ready for the placement of the images in the insets.

FOURTH VARIANT
Windows

For windowed pages, sets of cut-out boards are hinged and folded and the image material is sandwiched between the sets.

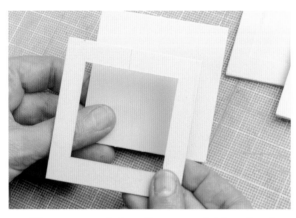

30. The mat is made by adhering a solid board and a window together.

33. The pair of windows is attached to the hinge material. The joint width is the thickness of the board.

31. After attaching the boards to the covering material, I cut an X into the inset that allows the cloth to move, so I can work the cloth up against the board edges. Then I attach hinged pairs together as described in step 15 on page 213.

34. The pairs are folded so that the hinge material is on the outside.

35. Then the images are attached to the outside of the folded pair.

36. To adhere the next pair, I sandwich the image material between the two.

37. The finished model.

Hinging Accordion Folds

Using the stiff-leaf hinging structure for accordion-fold books provides great opportunities for open display. For this example, four pairs are hinged together. One is solid, one is a mat, and two are windows. Attach any image materials before assembling into the book form. Take care in laying out the order of the pages since it's easy to get this mixed up.

38. The pages are layed out in order, with the pages they will be attached to above them. The joint width is three times the board thickness. The hinges are adhered to both edges of each page, except the first and last page, which only have a hinge on the inner edge.

39. Once the lower boards are hinged, I attach the corresponding pages. Weighting the boards during the work helps adhesion and alignment.

40. Once all boards are attached, I fold the book, place wax paper between the pages, and dry it under a weight. The finished model is shown on the following page.

About the Artist

JULIE LEONARD is a book artist working in Iowa City, IA, teaching book arts and graphic design at the University of Iowa's Center for the Book and School of Art and Art History. After obtaining a B.A. in History from Vassar College, she studied book design and illustration at the New England School of Art and Design. While working as a book designer, she began to explore book structures, decorative paper techniques and hand papermaking.

In 1989, she went to Penland School of Crafts as a fellowship student in book arts and papermaking. She was awarded an artist-in-residence position at Penland for the years 1990 to 1993 and was studio coordinator for the book, paper, and drawing studios during that time. In 1997, she moved to Iowa City and received an M.F.A. in

design and a Graduate Certificate in Book Arts from the University of Iowa.

Julie shows her work nationally, most recently at the Bright Hill Press Annual Book Arts Show, St. Louis Artist's Guild, and University of Wyoming Art Museum, Reynolds Gallery, CA, and Arts Iowa City. Her work is in permanent collections including University of Delaware Special Collections Library, Ringling School of Art and Design, The Sackner Archive of Visual and Concrete Poetry. She also exhibits in juried craft shows including the Philadelphia Craft Show, The Smithsonian Craft Show, American Craft Exposition, various American Craft Enterprises shows, and Crafts at the Castle in Boston.

In addition to teaching at the Universitiy of Iowa, she has taught at Penland School of Crafts, Omega Institute for Holistic Studies, and a number of art centers. She has been a visiting artist and teacher in the public schools in North Carolina and Iowa.

Gallery

The artists represented here approach the book very differently. What they hold in common for me is a wonderful sensitivity in choosing materials and how they weave content and form together. This work requires the a settling in, with its looking and looking again, that gives good book art its particular power.

Pam Spitzmueller's work builds on her great interest and expertise in historical book structures and materials. This knowledge allows her to make contemporary works with a sense of timelessness. The tactile qualities she incorporates are as compelling as the visual, demanding the reader both handles the book and looks at it closely.

Bonnie Stablecker's work, with its strong imagery and imaginative structures, presents personal subject matter in a way that lets the reader in. Her work usually contains a strong sense of narrative; personal tales that expand to include the world. Her sensitivity to format and materials gives Bonnie's books a particular grace.

A Modern Symposium by Christina Shmigel and Holly Ewald is a collaborative piece using an existing text. Working over a period of five years, the two artists, responded to the pages done by the other using drawing, collage, and cutouts to create the pages. The intimacy of the relationship between the two artists is felt on every page. Their use of an old book rather than a blank sketchbook adds to the feeling of lives lived, memories, dreams, and experience as they occur and pass on.

Shanna Leino's work, with her innate understanding of materials, allows her to combine unusual structures and materials in a way that enhances both. Storm in Kentucky is a great example. Metal, paper, text, and image blend so beautifully, one cannot imagine another solution. As with Pam's work, there's a tactility that calls out to the hands.

Shanna Leino, *The Devil's Charms,* 1999. 2½ x 3 inches (6.4 x 7.6 cm). Brass, linen thread. *Photos by Walker Montgomery.*

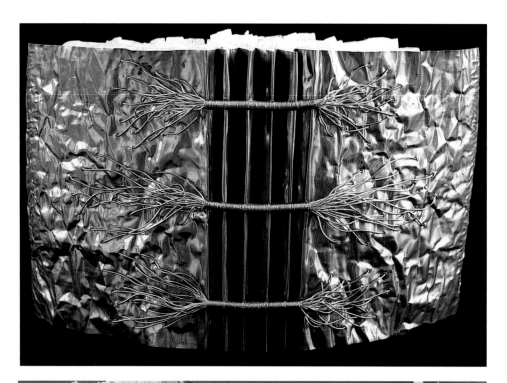

Pamela Spitzmueller, *British Museum Memoir-Copper Book,* 1999. 5 x 9 x 4½ inches (12.7 x 22.9 x 11.4 cm). Typewriter text and hand-drawn color pencil imagery; cover is one sheet of copper, crumpled and pleated with concertina folds; clear fishing line attaches book to wrapped cooper wires. *Photo by the artist.*

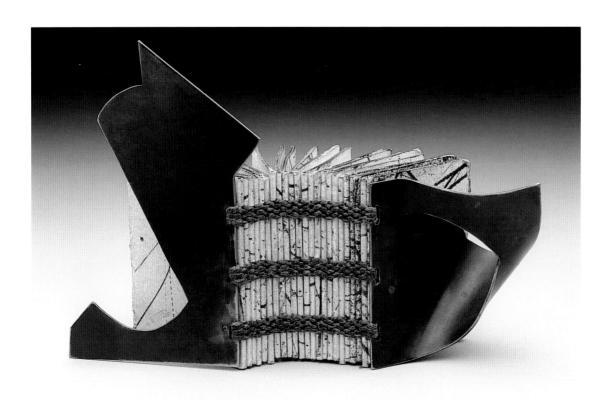

Hills and heat and
ticks and thunder,

Shanna Leino, *Storm in Kentucky,* 1998.3½ x 2 inches (8.9 x 5 cm). Brass, flax paper, linen thread; letterpress printed. *Photo by Walker Montgomery.*

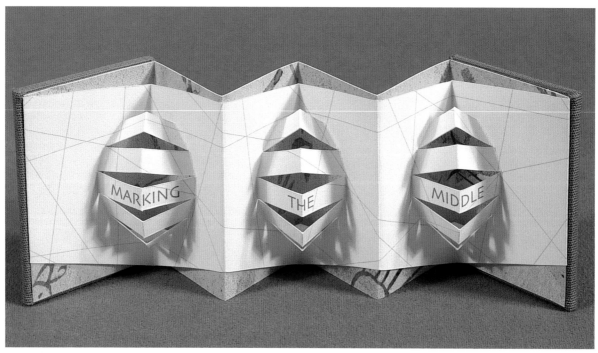

Bonnie Stahlecker, *Mid Point,* 2001. 2⁵⁄₁₆ x 1¹¹⁄₁₆ inches (5.8 x 4.2 cm). Ink jet printed with pop-up construction. *Photo by the artist.*

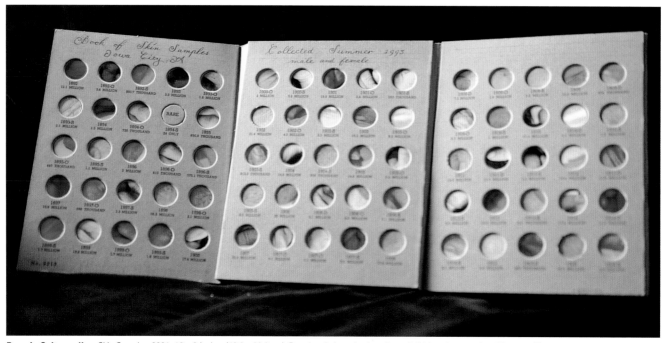

Pamela Spitzmueller, *Skin Samples,* 2001. 19 x 8 inches (48.3 x 20.3 cm). Found and altered coin collector's folder, photographs of human skin. *Photo by the artist.*

JULIE LEONARD

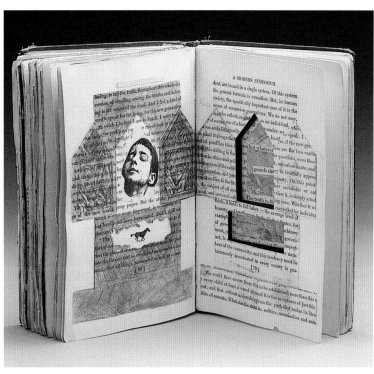

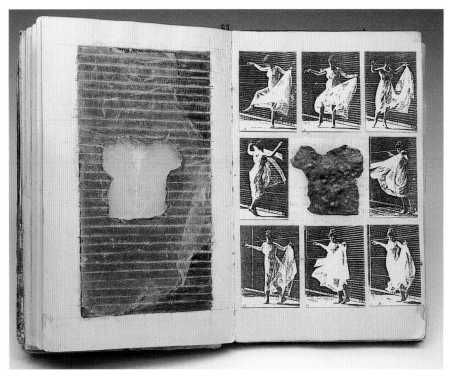

Christina Shmigel and Holly Ewald,
A Modern Symposium, 1987-1994. 5 x 7½ x
1 inches (12.7 x 19 x 2.5 cm). Collage, drawings; altered book, mailed back and forth
between NYC and Louisiana. Each artist
worked on three verso pages to initiate a
collaborative spread and three recto pages
to respond. Portions of pages cut to high-
light phrases of original text, its meaning
altered by its new context. *Photos by Tom Mills
and Cathy Carver.*

A Short History of Penland School of Crafts

Penland School of Crafts is a national center for craft education, located in the mountains of North Carolina. Penland's mission is to promote individual and artistic growth through crafts. The school hosts one-, two-, and eight-week workshops in books and paper, clay, drawing and painting, glass, iron, metals, photography, printmaking, textiles, and wood. The school also sponsors artists' residencies, a community education program, and a craft gallery representing artists affiliated with the school.

Penland was founded by Lucy Morgan, a teacher at an Episcopalian school that once occupied several buildings which are still part of Penland. In 1923, she organized the Penland Weavers, to provide looms and materials, instruct local women, and establish a market their handwoven goods. She invited noted weaving expert Edward F. Worst to teach, and when requests for instruction came from other parts of the country, Penland School was born. Soon after the first students arrived in 1929, other crafts were added, and the school began to raise funds, acquire property, and construct buildings.

When Lucy Morgan retired in 1962, she was succeeded by Bill Brown. During Brown's 21-year tenure, new media, such as iron and glass, were added to the program, and the school began offering eight-week sessions in the spring and fall. Brown also started the resident artist program, which provides low-cost housing and studios to craft artists who work at Penland for several years, and he began a work-study scholarship program to make Penland accessible to a broader range of students.

Today the school encompasses six buildings located on 400 acres of land. Each year approximately 1,200 people come to Penland for instruction and another 12,000 pass through as visitors. The community education program brings first-hand craft experience to hundreds of local school children.

Penland has no standing faculty; its instructors include full-time studio artists as well as teachers from colleges and universities. Students live at Penland and take only one class at a time, allowing them to learn by total immersion—the ideas and information gained in a two-week session can take a year to absorb and process.

The school has also become the focal point for a lively community of craft artists, thanks in part to the resident program, which has encouraged many artists to settle in the area. The presence of so many nearby studios greatly enhances the quality of the student experience.

Students come from all walks of life. They range from 19 to 90 years of age and from absolute beginners to professional craftspeople. Some see Penland as a productive retreat, some as a source of inspiration for their personal creative life, and others as a place to exchange vital information about material, technique, and process.

What brings them all together is a love of materials and making, and the often transformative experience of working with intensity and focus in a supportive community atmosphere.

Robin Dreyer

Acknowledgments

Lark Books is proud to present *The Penland Book of Handmade Books* as the second in a series of collaborations with Penland School of Crafts. The completion of such a complex project is truly a team effort. It is through the extraordinary contributions made by the wonderful people connected to Penland that we have been able to bring this book to fruition.

Recognition, first, must go to the artists Carol Barton, Jim Croft, Dan Essig, Susan E. King, Hedi Kyle, Julie Leonard, Barbara Mauriello, Steve Miller, Dolph Smith, and Eileen Wallace. Their enthusiastic willingness to commit to the book is inspiring. Not only did they endure the pressure of meeting publishing deadlines to deliver both written and visual material, they did so while teaching workshops, lecturing, exhibiting, and continuing to produce their own creative work. It is in light of their hard work, dedication, talent, and cheerful attitudes that we say you were all a joy to work with—we applaud you.

Jean McLaughlin, Director of Penland School of Crafts, enthusiastically endorsed the book and other key Penland staff members were instrumental in bringing the book to publication. Our thanks go to the steady hand of Dana Moore, Penland Program Director. She made the initial contacts with the artists, acted as the school's liaison throughout the many months of production, and reviewed the manuscript. Robin Dreyer, Communications Manager, also provided much helpful insight with his manuscript review. Rory Golden, Executive Director of The Center for Book Arts in New York City, and Anna Embree, Assistant Professor of Book Arts at the University of Alabama in Tuscaloosa, Alabama, took time to act as technical manuscript consultants.

Lark Books art director Celia Naranjo, along with photographer Steve Mann and a number of other photographers around the U.S., helped shape the book's unique visual look. Special thanks also goes to assistant editor Rebecca Lim for her steadfast help.

JANE LAFERLA
VERONIKA ALICE GUNTER
Editors

For more information about Penland School of Crafts, call (828) 765-2359 or visit www. penland.org

Contributing Photographers

RALPH BARTHOLDT of St. Maries, Idaho, photographed
Jim Croft at his home workshop.

TERESA GOLSON of Tuscaloosa, Alabama, took the portrait
and Hands On photos for Steve Miller in his studio at the
University of Alabama.

JILL MICHKA of Carlville, Iowa, took the photos for
Julie Leonard at the University of Iowa in Iowa City.

SEAN MOSER of New York, New York, photographed
Barbara Mauriello in her Hoboken, New Jersey, studio.

ANTHONY PERITORE, of Picture That Studio in Falls
Church, Virginia, photographed Carol Barton at work in
her studio.

MURRAY RISS of Memphis, Tennessee, photographed Dolph
Smith's portrait in Dolph's studio.

DEBORAH ROUNDTREE of Emeryville, California,
photographed Susan E. King's Hands On section and portrait.

PAUL WARCHOL of Paul Warchol Photography New York,
New York, photographed Hedi Kyle's portrait and her work
in progress.

Contributing Artists

CAROL BARTON
Glen Echo, MD, USA
Page 134

TERRY BRAUNSTEIN
Long Beach, CA, USA
Pages 109, 111, 112

MEREDITH BRICKELL
Lincoln, NE, USA
Page 28

INGE BRUGGEMAN
Portland, OR, USA
Page 66

DENISE CARBONE
Stratford, NJ, USA
Pages 130, 135

SQUEAK CARNWATH
Oakland, CA, USA
Page 46

THOMAS ELIOT CONROY
Berkeley, CA, USA
Page 196

BETSY DAVIDS
Berkeley, CA, USA
Page 112

WILLIAM DRENDEL
Chicago, IL, USA
Pages 67, 133, 175, 181

DANIEL ESSIG
Asheville, NC, USA
Page 179

HOLLY EWALD
Page 223

HOSS HALEY
Asheville, NC, USA
Pages 30, 45

SJOERD HOFSTRA
Brooklyn, NY, USA
Page 87

HEDI KYLE
Philadelphia, PA, USA
Pages 151, 153, 198

RUTH LAXSON
Atlanta, GA, USA
Page 113

SHANNA LEINO
Harrisville, NH, USA
Pages 28, 219, 221

Mick LeTourneaux
Princeton, NJ, USA
Page 47

KEITH LO BUE
Pages 25, 26

JOAN LYONS
Rochester, NY, USA
Page 108

PETER MADDEN
Boston, MA, USA
Page 110

EMILY MARTIN
Iowa City, IA, USA
Pages 84, 85, 88, 128-129, 135

BARBARA MAURIELLO
Hoboken, NJ, USA
Page 132

SCOTT MCCARNEY
Rochester, NY, USA
Pages 108, 133, 134

RICHARD MINSKY
Hudson, NY, USA
Page 154

LOIS MORRISON
Leonia, NJ, USA
Page 86

KATHERINE NG
Los Angeles, CA, USA
Page 108

KURT NIELSEN
Belmont, NC, USA
Page 29

BONNIE O'CONNELL
Omaha, NE, USA
Pages 109, 110

ROBYN RAINES
Philadelphia, PA, USA
Pages 26, 30

CHRIS RAMSAY
Stillwater, OK, USA
Pages 27, 31

HARRY REESE
Isla Vista, CA, USA
Page 67

BILLY RILEY
Page 180

KATHERINE MCCANLESS RUFFIN
Wellesley, MA, USA
Page 67

CHRISTINA SHMIGEL
St. Louis, MO, USA
Page 223

ROBBIN AMI SILVERBERG
Pages 178, 181
Brooklyn, NY, USA

ALLISON SMITH
New York, NY, USA
Pages 177, 178, 179

DOLPH SMITH
Ripley, TN, USA
Page 31

PAMELA SPITZMUELLER
Medford, MA, USA
Pages 28, 132, 152, 197, 199,
220, 222

BROOK SPURLOCK
CA, USA
Page 30

BONNIE STAHLECKER
Plainfield, IN, USA
Pages 66, 86, 87, 177, 222

C. CHRISTOPHER STERN
Sedro-Woolley, WA, USA
Pages 64-65

LYNN SURES
Wheaton, MD, USA
Pages 174, 176

FRANCES L. SWEDLUND
Cobden, IL. USA
Page 27

MATTHEW THOMASON
Bakersville, NC, USA
Page 28

CLAIRE VAN VLIET
Newark, VT, USA
Page 131

LAURA WAIT
Denver, CO, USA
Pages 44, 45

ROBERT WARNER
New York, NY, USA
Pages 150, 153, 155

DOROTHY YULE
Oakland, CA, USA
Pages 85, 89

PHILIP ZIMMERMANN
Rhinebeck, NY, USA
Page 106, 107

Index